Fleeting Impressions

PRINTS BY JAMES MCNEILL WHISTLER

PRINTS BY JAMES MCNEILL WHISTLER

Fleeting Impressions: Prints by James McNeill Whistler was published on the occasion of the exhibition of the same name originated by the Montgomery Museum of Fine Arts, Montgomery, Alabama, and on view there March 25 through May 21, 2006.

Library of Congress Cataloging-in-Publication Data
Whistler, James McNeill, 1834-1903.
Fleeting impressions: prints by James McNeill Whistler.
p.cm.
Catalog of an exhibition at the Montgomery Museum of Fine Arts, Montgomery, AL March 25-May 21 2006.
Includes bibliographical references.
ISBN 0-89280-049-6
1. Whistler, James McNeill, 1834-1903--Exhibitions. I. Montgomery Museum of Fine Arts. II. Title.
NE539.W5A4 2006

769.92--dc22

2005038009

ISBN: 0-89280-049-6

Catherine E. Hutchins, *Editor*
Leigh Hillabrand, Camille Leonard, and Mary Catherine Phillips, *LWT Communications, Design and Production*
Emily Stuart Thomas, *Montgomery Museum of Fine Arts, Photographer*
Skinner Printing, Printer

Cover illustration: *The Riva, No. 2* (Detail), Checklist of the Exhibition No. 46

Fleeting Impressions

PRINTS BY JAMES MCNEILL WHISTLER

Montgomery Museum of Fine Arts

Acknowledgements

The Board and Staff of the Montgomery Museum of Fine Arts express their most sincere appreciation to the following individuals who participated in the organization and realization of this exhibition:

Mrs. Adolph Weil, Jr., Montgomery, Alabama

Eric Denker, Washington, D.C.

Jennifer Fleming, Baltimore, Maryland

Emilie K. Johnson, North Adams, Massachusetts

Josephine W. Rodgers, San Francisco, California

LENDERS TO THE EXHIBITION
The Trout Gallery, Dickinson College, Carlisle, Pennsylvania

EXHIBITION SPONSORS
General Casualty Insurance Company
Morgan Stanley
Summit America, LLC

CATALOGUE SPONSOR
Mrs. Adolph Weil, Jr.

The Montgomery Museum of Fine Arts, a department of the City of Montgomery, is supported by funds from the City and County of Montgomery and the Montgomery Museum of Fine Arts Association. Programs are made possible, in part, by grants from the Alabama State Council on the Arts and the National Endowment for the Arts.

Table of Contents

Foreword

James McNeill Whistler's colorful personality and his artistic career were uniquely his own, but equally they reflect a momentous era in world history. Societies in the late-nineteenth-century underwent a scientific, economic, and cultural transformation, evolving from a reliance on convention to a hunger for experimentation and change they confidently identified as "progress." These societies rapidly manifested the now familiar mindsets of modernity with Western Europe and the United States as leading players in this transformation. Whistler, an American émigré who lived his eventful life on the European stage, gained as much notoriety as renown. Equal parts triumph and pathos, his fascinating life story has engaged several generations of biographers and scholars. Historic perspective, however, reveals a much larger legacy: that, in keeping with this era of change, Whistler was an artist of profound importance to the development of the aesthetic foundations of twentieth-century art.

This exhibition of sixty three etchings, drypoints, and lithographs by Whistler from the collection of the Montgomery Museum of Fine Arts constitutes the third in a series founded upon the museum's holdings of Old Master prints acquired through the generosity of Adolph (Bucks) Weil, Jr. Appropriately enough, the first exhibition ("Rembrandt, Beyond the Brush," 1999) focused upon the print work of Rembrandt van Rijn, a seventeenth-century Dutch painter/printmaker whose work inspired Whistler. The second exhibition ("Faith and Humanism," 2002) examined the roots of printmaking in Western Europe as provided by Albrecht Dürer. From his work grew an expansive and flourishing tradition that produced a rich heritage for many late-nineteenth-century printmakers, including Whistler. It is appropriate that the third in this series of exhibitions examines the prints of an artist who brought this tradition to fruition and propelled it forward into the modern era.

As guest curator Eric Denker makes clear in his insightful essay for this catalogue, even while being innovative, Whistler drew upon sources of inspiration that had roots in the past. Mr. Denker deftly presents the abundant scholarship on Whistler's career as he demonstrates the breadth of Whistler's achievement and explains the importance of understanding Whistler's artistic vision in order to appreciate the art movements that followed. The museum is fortunate to have such an outstanding representation of the works of Whistler, who truly serves as a bridge between traditional and modern art.

The prints of Whistler were abiding favorites of Bucks Weil, and he pursued them assiduously with the intention that the museum would build a substantial collection. While his true loves were the prints of the fourteenth to the eighteenth centuries, Mr. Weil believed that the museum's American collection would be incomplete without the ability to demonstrate the abundant talents of this colorful painter/printmaker. He encouraged an appreciation of Whistler's work and its use as an educational tool for connecting American art to its roots in Western European traditions.

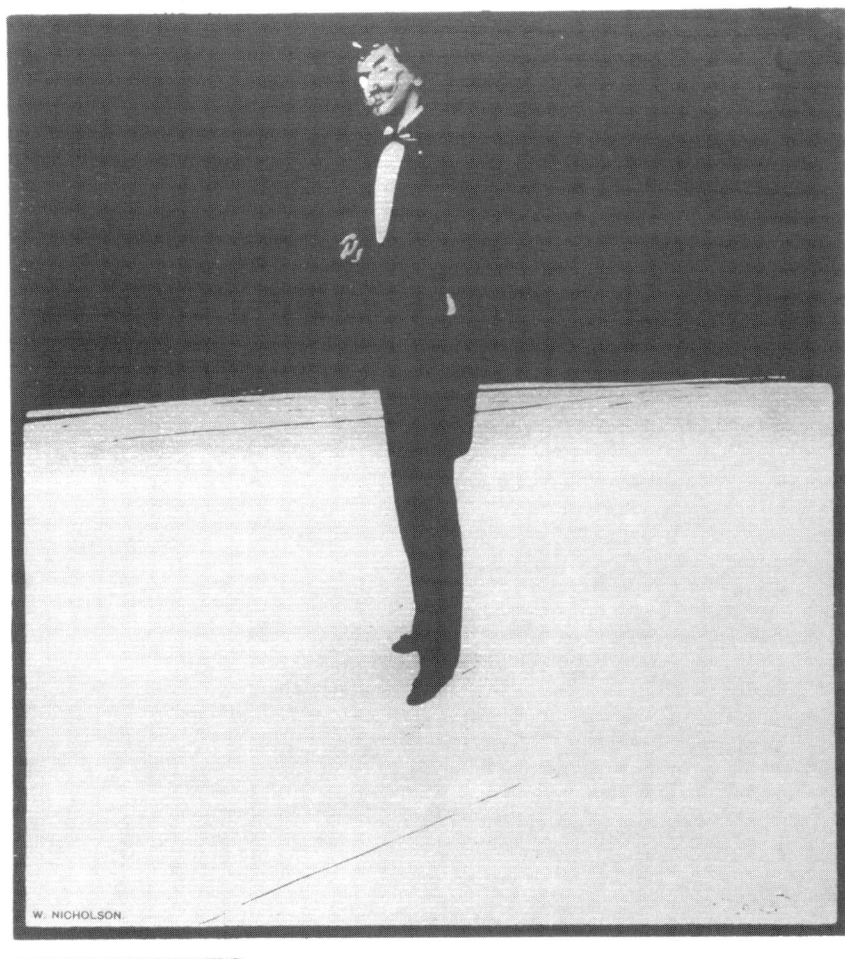

Portrait of Whistler, c. 1898
Sir William Nicolson (English, 1872-1949)
Lithograph on paper
The Trout Gallery, Dickinson College, Carlisle, Pennsylvania

The museum continues to build upon the foundation established by Bucks Weil, developing the print collection as an integral part of the museum's holdings. As has been noted previously, he charted a course for our collections that has paid outstanding dividends in our ability to teach about art and its history.

We continue to be profoundly grateful to Bucks's wife, Jean Weil, for her ongoing support of this series of exhibitions that document the legacy Bucks provided his hometown museum. The scholarship of Eric Denker and contributors Emilie K. Johnson and Josephine W. Rodgers joins the wealth of documentation that has been provided for our print collection over the past seven years by prominent experts in the history of prints and printmaking. We appreciate their dedication and creativity in seeing that the work is properly identified and interpreted. Montgomery Museum of Fine Arts staff members, especially Curator Margaret Lynne Ausfeld, Registrar Pamela Bransford, Photographer Emily Stuart Thomas, and Preparator Jeff Dutton, organized the exhibition and coordinated the preparation of the catalogue. Our editor, Catherine Hutchins, and designers at LWT Communications did their usual outstanding jobs in seeing this volume to completion. We appreciate the efforts of all concerned to make these wonderful works of art more accessible to our audience and to scholars worldwide.

Mark M. Johnson, DIRECTOR

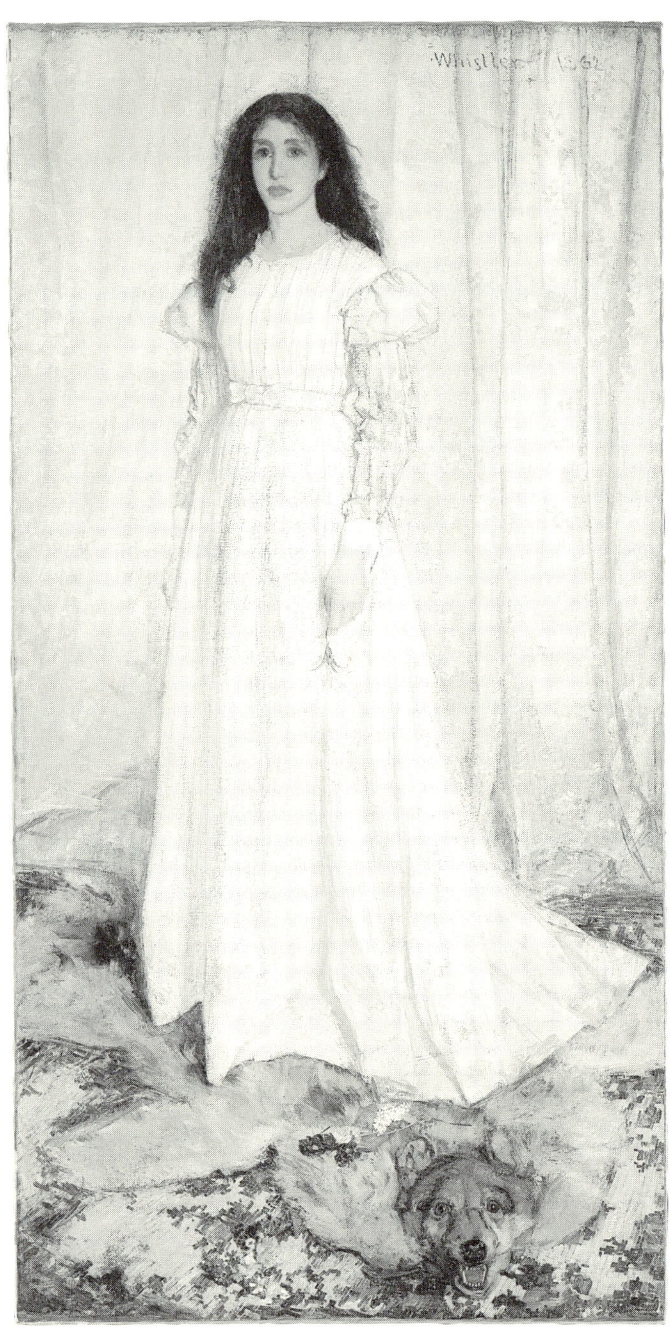

FIGURE 1

Symphony in White, No. 1: The White Girl, 1863
Oil on canvas
National Gallery of Art, Washington, D.C.
Harris Whittemore Collection
1943.6.2

Whistler and the Search for Printed Tone

WHISTLER'S PLACE IN NINETEENTH CENTURY ART

American expatriate James McNeill Whistler is as elusive to fully grasp today as he was difficult to categorize during his long and innovative career. He was a significant painter, printmaker, and theoretician whose work is recognized as an important achievement in nineteenth-century art, but whose importance as a precursor of twentieth-century art movements remains undervalued. Whistler, in both his work and his writing, deserves to be mentioned with the same veneration generally reserved for Manet and Cézanne, as a radical reformer of the pictorial arts and a pioneer in the development of nonrepresentational art. Yet, because his work does not fit comfortably into one of the major, easily defined, and popular movements of the later nineteenth century, scholars regularly give him short shrift. Aesthetically, Whistler always pursued his own single-minded vision of art. This has led to one of the supreme ironies of art history—although the gregarious painter both craved and received enormous attention in England, France, and the United States during his lifetime, his unique development and achievement has placed him outside the accepted narrative of the history of art.

Whistler always receives scant attention in the general overviews of Western art, and even most surveys of nineteenth-century painting, owing to the difficulty in placing his work in a particular category or movement.[1] In this he is not unlike Jean-Baptiste-Camille Corot, who often receives less than his due recognition since he is not easily identifiable as a late romantic painter, a Barbizon artist, or a realist landscape painter. Occasionally, Whistler's *Symphony in White, No. 1: The White Girl* (FIG. 1) is illustrated in a survey, but mostly for its political role in the Salon des Refusés. More often the authors choose the familiar *Arrangement in Gray and Black, No. 1: Portrait of the Artist's Mother* (FIG. 2) and one of the landscape nocturnes of the 1870s, sometimes *Nocturne in Blue and Gold: Old Battersea Bridge* or occasionally *Nocturne in Black and Gold: The Falling Rocket* (FIG. 3), either of which allows for a discussion of Whistler's 1878 lawsuit against art critic John Ruskin. In a consideration of the increasing role of formal analysis in aesthetics, authors are often discomforted by both the inclusion and the placement of Whistler. The problem is understandable—if Cézanne receives credit as the revolutionary who wrenched Western painting away from an addiction to representation in the 1880s, how does one deal with Whistler's canvasses and aesthetic theories that teeter on the definition of abstraction, such as this one, in the 1870s:

> My picture of a "Harmony in Grey and Gold" is an illustration of my meaning—a snow scene with a single black figure and a lighted tavern. I care nothing for the past, present, or future of the black figure, placed

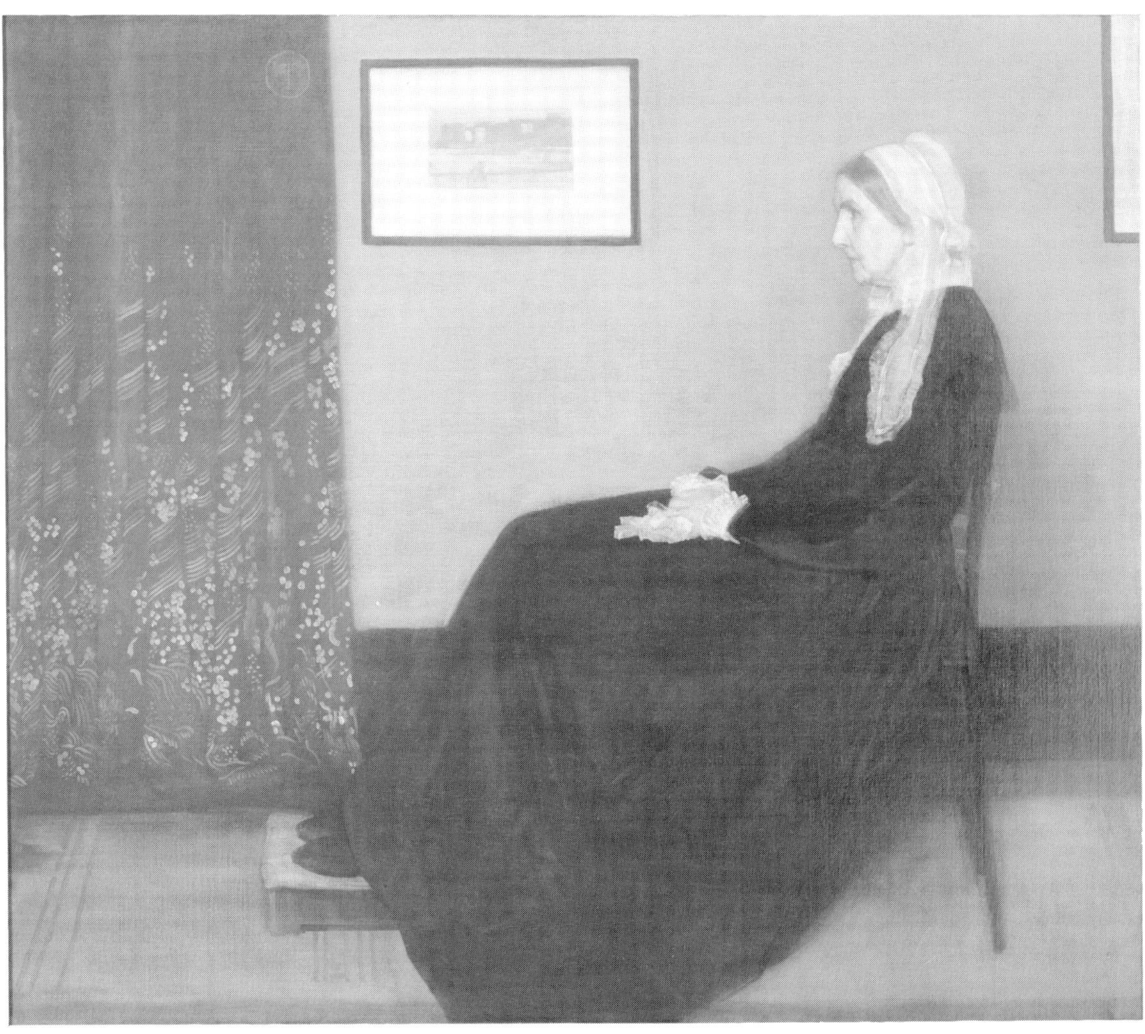

FIGURE 2

Arrangement in Gray and Black, No. 1: Portrait of the Artist's Mother, 1871
Oil on canvas
Musee d'Orsay, Paris, France

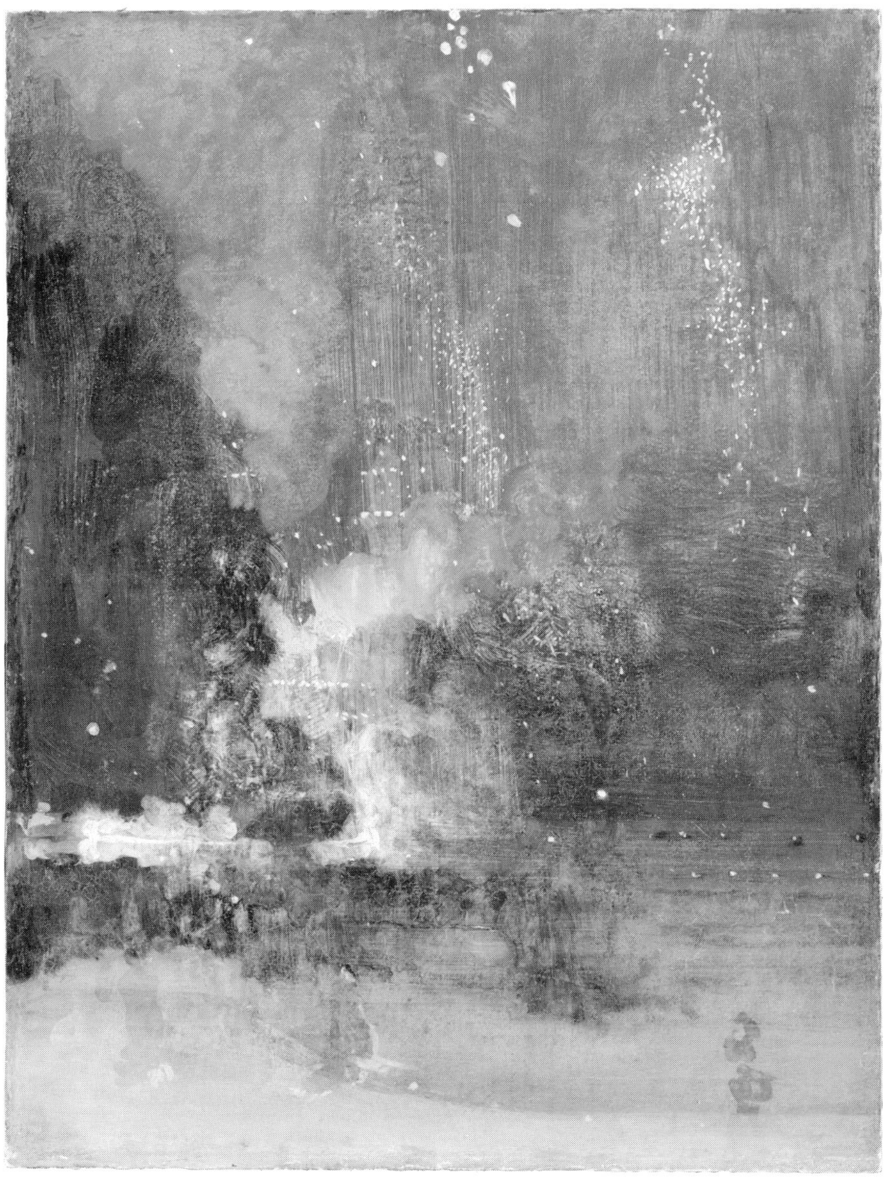

FIGURE 3

Nocturne in Black and Gold: The Falling Rocket, c.1875
Oil on panel
The Detroit Institute of Arts, USA
Gift of Dexter M. Ferry Jr.

there because black was wanted at that spot. All that I know is that my combination of grey and black is the basis of the picture... As music is the poetry of sound, so is painting the poetry of sight, and the subject-matter has nothing to do with harmony of sound or of colour.[2]

By limiting themselves in defining the position of Whistler, scholars find themselves in a situation similar to the celebrated Indostan blind men and the elephant in the poem of John Godfrey Saxe, an American of Whistler's era; each seizes on one salient feature to the exclusion of the larger story.[3] With Whistler, the difficulties increase when scholars approach the questions of nationality and style. Americans claim Whistler because he was born in Massachusetts to American parents, and because he always retained his identification as an American, as an outsider living in a hostile British artistic environment.[4] Yet, equally, he might be claimed by France, where he formed his aesthetic opinions in the cauldron of French theory at midcentury and where his most significant training occurred. Or yet again, he might be (and often is) included in a survey of nineteenth-century art in Britain, where he lived for the overwhelming majority of his adult life. It is prudent to recall that Whistler spent only fifteen of his first twenty-one years in the United States, never returning to this side of the Atlantic after attaining his majority. By a similar formulation, writers might admit the right of Greece to claim El Greco, of Italy to claim John Singer Sargent, of England to claim Thomas Moran, and of Denmark to celebrate Camille Pissarro, who was born and raised in Danish territory and retained his nationality throughout his life.

We encounter added difficulties in identifying Whistler with a particular group among the avant-garde in France and England. He received his most serious training in France in the heyday of Gustave Courbet and his revolutionary promotion of realism, but Whistler worked only briefly as a realist in painting and only a bit longer in printmaking. He retained his youthful friendships with Edouard Manet, Claude Monet, Edgar Degas, Camille Pissarro, and many of the impressionists, but his work is impressionist only in a few etchings and in a very limited sense of the word. He spent most of his life working in England during the Victorian era, but scholars are reticent to refer to him as either English or Victorian, particularly given his own aversion to both labels. He became close friends with John Everett Millais, Dante Gabriel Rossetti, and the members of the Pre-Raphaelite Brotherhood, but his work never engaged their ideals. Although friends of French symbolist artists and writers, including Stéphane Mallarmé, and later a supporter of Pierre Bonnard and Edouard Vuillard and the Nabi circle, he did not identify closely with these French modernist groups. We are left with a generic description: Whistler was born in the United States, and called himself American but was a French-trained artist working in England in the second half of the nineteenth century. Yet that simple formulation ignores Whistler's international importance in setting the stage for nonrepresentational art and minimizes his tremendous influence on principles of abstraction in the twentieth-century.

And so these men of Indostan
Disputed loud and long,
Each in his own opinion
Exceeding stiff and strong,
Though each was partly in the right,
And all were in the wrong![5]

THE QUEST FOR TONALITY

The problem of categorization that plagues Whistler as a painter is not considered as serious a detriment in appreciating his career as a printmaker. Influential writer Charles-Pierre Baudelaire commended Whistler's talent in that realm in 1862. "Just the other day a young American artist, M. Whistler, was showing at the Galerie Martinet a set of etchings, as subtle and lively as improvisation and inspiration, representing the banks of the Thames, wonderful tangles of rigging, yardarms and rope; farragos of fog, furnaces and corkscrews of smoke; the profound and intricate poetry of a vast capital."[6]

Four years prior to that, in spring 1859, Whistler's prints won acceptance at the Salon in Paris and at the Royal Academy in London. In Paris he exhibited two realist images he had executed the previous year, one identifiable as *La Marchande de Moutarde* (The Mustard Merchant); in London he exhibited two unidentified works. In the 1860s, even when Whistler's paintings met with mixed reception, and regular rejection from both the Academy and the Salon, critics simultaneously acknowledged his strengths as a draftsman and a consummate etcher. From the outset of his career, Whistler conceived of much of his graphic work in terms of sets, to be presented and marketed as groups of related images, inspired by both the vogue for Japanese woodblock prints, and the recognized master of the revival of etching, Charles Meryon. By 1860 Whistler had already executed one set of etchings, the French Set, and planned a second set, which would not be published for another decade, several years before the burgeoning revival of etching led to the Société des Aquafortistes and its annual volume of etchings. His earliest important prints were included in "Twelve Etchings from Nature" of 1858, generally referred to as the French Set. He was planning a second set at the time of his immigration to England, although his "Sixteen Etchings of Scenes of the Thames," referred to as the Thames Set, was not issued until 1871. Later, he went to Venice in September 1879 with the explicit commission to render a set of twelve etchings of the city in a brief three month period. That three month period stretched to fourteen, during which he executed a sufficient number to publish both the original dozen, the First Venice Set, and a second series of mostly Venetian scenes, the Second Venice Set. A decade later, in 1889, he traveled to Amsterdam, the city of his artistic idol Rembrandt van Rijn, where he planned and executed the Amsterdam Set, which the Fine Art Society, a commercial enterprise and the publisher of the First Venice Set, declined to handle. The artist also completed a set of twelve prints in one day that he sent to Queen Victoria as a Jubilee present. Although this last series, a slight achievement, remains unrepresented in the collection of the Montgomery Museum of Fine Arts, a majority of the prints in the collection are from the earlier series: three from the French Set; the complete series of the Thames Set, though from different stages in the evolution of the plates; ten of the First Venice Set; eight of the Second Venice Set; and one from the Amsterdam Set. Even in his early lithographs Whistler thought in terms of series, and several of the sheets in this exhibition derive from the Notes that Whistler's printer Thomas Way encouraged him to publish in 1878. An assessment of Whistler's maturation as a printmaker and his ongoing quest for tone in his prints is possible through an examination and discussion of the chronology and characteristics of each set in the artist's career.

A few biographical notes provide the necessary grounding for the analysis of Whistler's development as a printmaker. On July 11, 1834, Whistler was born in Lowell, Massachusetts, a fact he regularly attempted to obscure for much of the rest of his life.[7] George Washington Whistler, the artist's father, was a civil engineer in the United States Army. In 1842, Major Whistler accepted the invitation of Nicholas I, czar of Russia, to design and build the first railway line from Moscow to St. Petersburg. The family followed the Major to Russia a year later, and the young James spent much of the next six years in St. Petersburg, taking his first art lessons at the Imperial Academy of Fine Arts. His hosts at the Russian court, a cultivated and cosmopolitan circle in which French was spoken, regarded James as the child of an honored visitor. He appears to have been shaped in some ways by his experience during these formative years—he received a broad education, became familiar with art, and although often the center of attention, became accustomed to thinking of himself as an outsider. He also had the opportunity to spend time in London with his brother-in-law Francis Seymour Haden, a doctor, an amateur etcher, and an astute collector. The death of Major Whistler in April 1849 necessitated the family's relocation to Pomfret, Connecticut. Two years later, the young artist followed in his father's footsteps and entered the United States Military Academy at West Point, then under Colonel Robert E. Lee. Whistler excelled at drawing in classes taught by Robert W. Weir but exhibited a notable lack of discipline in his other coursework, which led to his dismissal from the academy in June 1854. After a short apprenticeship at Thomas Winan's locomotive works in Baltimore, he arrived in Washington in November with an appointment to the United States Coast and Geodetic Survey. He lasted there for less than two months, making it just into the New Year before being summarily dismissed for bad work habits and lack of attendance. Though his period at the Geodetic Survey was brief, it proved crucial to his later development, since this is where he experienced his first serious exposure to etching and learned to etch. A classmate and colleague, John Ross Key, later described their introduction to printmaking:

> Mr. McCoy, one of the best engravers in the office, a kindly, genial Irishman, always ready to aid or advise the younger men, listened while I explained our mission. He then went over the whole process with us—how to prepare the copper plate, how to put on the ground, and how to smoke dark, so that the lines made by the point could be plainly seen.
>
> For the first time since his entrance into the office Whistler was intently interested. Always sedate, he was also singularly indifferent, but on this occasion he seemed to realize that a new medium for the expression of his artistic sense was being put within his grasp. He listened attentively to McCoy's somewhat wordy explanations, asked a few questions, and squinted inquisitively through his half-closed eyes at the sample of work placed before him. Having been provided with a copper plate such as was kept for the use of beginners, and an etching point, he started off to make his first experiment as an etcher.[8]

While at the Geodetic Survey, he executed several plates, including *Sketches on the Coast Survey Plate* (CHECKLIST 1). The twenty-year-old novice painstakingly rendered the landscape of Anacapa Island, and then added several large fantasy heads to the scene. Short parallel strokes indicate the contours of the landscape but crosshatching, a technique Whistler had learned in Weir's drawing classes at the academy, is limited to the modeling of the heads. Six months later, in July 1855, Whistler turned twenty one, at which point he began receiving an income from his father's estate, and soon thereafter moved to Paris to study art, leaving the United States never to return.

In France Whistler enrolled at the Ecole Impériale et Spéciale de Dessin, followed by study in the atelier of Swiss academician, Charles Gleyre, where he received his first training as a painter. He also engaged in the time-honored tradition of learning through copying in the Louvre. At the same time as he was studying old master painting, however, he was inspired by Courbet's contemporary approach to realism, and his early drawings reflect this modernist vocabulary. Whistler's first series of etchings, the French Set, constitutes a realist venture, as *Street at Saverne* (CAT. ENTRY 1, P. 25), *La Veille aux Loques* (CHECKLIST 3), and *The Kitchen* (CAT. ENTRY 2, P. 27) demonstrate. *La Veille aux Loques* (The Old Rag Woman), a genre subject, presents a poor older woman sitting in the doorway of a humble dwelling. The tension between the two dimensionality of the image and the attempt at three-dimensional depth is rudimentary—we look from our space past a briefly described foreground into the darker recesses of the parallel space of the sitter. (Whistler wrestled with this tension between design and illusion throughout his career, resolving it in a variety of ways.) The draftsmanship, while confident, remained deliberately informal and sketchy. Heavily rendered areas of precise detail, such as the still-life elements on the shelf and wall behind the figure, sit beside broadly sketched areas that add nothing to the physical description of the elements of the composition. Whistler employed unusually dense crosshatching throughout the image, making it difficult to distinguish between the shadows and giving the plate a certain over-wrought appearance. Like the early works of many artists, whether in paint or print, this evinces a certain horror vacui on the part of a young practitioner who does not yet comprehend the balance of light and dark and the virtue of economy. The sketchiness clearly is reminiscent of Rembrandt's early works, which Whistler likely knew through Parisian dealers, impressions owned by his brother-in-law Francis Haden, and perhaps prints exhibited at the 1857 *Art Treasures* exhibition at Manchester that the young artist had attended. Whistler also handled the plate in a novice's way: haphazard fingerprints around the border detract from the image.

The same fingerprints are abundantly apparent in *The Kitchen* (CAT. ENTRY 2, P. 27), another heavily wrought image from the French Set. Here, in another realist subject, Whistler represented a woman seen from behind, silhouetted by a window at the far end of a deep space. Again, Whistler used dense networks of crosshatching and multiple hatching to create dark, murky areas of the composition, the shadowed interior walls meant to contrast and set off the brighter areas toward the window, and the silvery areas of the still life on the right side. Although he only etched one pure still life in the course of his career, *The Wine Glass*, Whistler had a wonderful eye for still-life details, as is obvious from the rendering of the stove and plates on the wall, the latter of which may have been inspired by the work of Venetian artist Paolo Veronese whose monumental *Supper in the House of Levi* hung in the Louvre.[9]

In perhaps the most significant of the plates from the French Set, the nocturnal *Street at Saverne* (CAT. ENTRY 1, P. 25), Whistler limited the heavy multiple hatching to the shadows dominating the lower left and center of the plate. However, Whistler was not entirely successful with either the recession of the buildings or with the shadows, which remain irreconcilable given the direction of the light. The MMFA print is a later impression on which he wiped the plate around the lamp to allow the strong contrast of the white of the paper to imitate the effect of bright light: areas of plate tone contrast with the cleanly wiped passages of the buildings on the left to create a brilliant contrast of cast light and dark shadow.

Whistler's second print set, "A Series of Sixteen Etchings of the Thames," published a dozen years later, brought together plates that he mostly had executed in 1859. His talents had blossomed in this series, demonstrating his greater confidence as a draftsman, greater sense of balance in design, and a greater command of economy in the details. In these, Whistler left behind the French and Rhine countryside with their sometimes heavily wrought figural scenes. Instead he concentrated on working-class life along the industrial lower Thames. According to Whistler's cover sheet to the series, the entries began with *Black Lion Wharf* (CHECKLIST 12).[10] Frederick Wedmore, the most important critic of contemporary printmaking in London during the 1870s, wrote "The portfolio opens with a characteristic specimen, *Black Lion Wharf*—a work decisive and precise in execution, emphatic where emphasis is needed, brilliant in contrast of dark and light, delicate in the handling of unobtrusive passages, slight and sketchy in the treatment of episode."[11]

Whistler celebrated the recognition of this etching by including it as the print on the wall in the back ground of the contemporary *Arrangement in Grey and Black, No. 1: Portrait of the Artist's Mother* (FIG. 2, P. 10). *Black Lion Wharf* is the only Whistler print to appear in one of the artist's own paintings. In some ways, this appears a curious choice, however, considering how Whistler clearly delighted in the most minute of details in the print, including the names of the various wharfs and shipping establishments. All of these crucial graphic elements are eliminated from the background of the painting, the etching reduced to the most basic geometry on the wall beyond the sitter.

Overall *Black Lion Wharf* constitutes one of Whistler's early masterpieces and is far more balanced and more restrained than the plates of the French Set. He controlled the sketchiness by containing it within the foreground costume and ropes. In the line of dilapidated buildings in the distance, he differentiated between the fabric and roof of each structure. He limited crosshatching to a few boats in the background, a few roofs, and a bit of foreground shadow. These rich areas contrast with the expanse of untouched paper that becomes, in the viewer's eyes, the sky above and the surface of the water below.

Throughout the series Whistler used the untouched areas of the plate as a foil of the heavily worked tone to give contrast and depth to his images. In *Thames Police* (CHECKLIST 14, P. 39) Whistler labored on the variety of walls and roofs throughout the background, alternating parallel lines and crosshatching, to create a mosaic of urban fabric, while limiting the sky to a few wispy lines to indicate clouds. In *Thames Warehouses* (CHECKLIST 7) he stippled and rouletted areas of the fore- and middle-ground boats on the left but limited the crosshatching to the extreme right and left of the plate, setting off the broad expanse of the calm river. *Limehouse* (CHECKLIST 9), a more complex plate, forces the viewer to engage the boat in the foreground without providing any immediate relief for the eye below the untouched sky. It, too, demonstrates Whistler's penchant for details: the writing on the walls. Other artists of the etching revival soon added legible signs to buildings in the middle- and background of a scene, including Maxime Lalanne in two noted images of the demolitions for new boulevards in Paris, and Francis Haden in *Yacht Tavern*.[12]

Whistler limited his hatching to the passages most needing of description, such as the wooden planking on the left side of *Limehouse* (CHECKLIST 9). He included a light veil of ink on the lower left to convey the fine, indistinct mist on the water. This tone contrasts with the clear sky above—Whistler rarely indicated clouds in any of the Thames Set. A careful examination of this impression reveals that one of Whistler's curly hairs fell on the plate during printing.

Whistler was not averse to using heavily hatched areas to imitate dark shadows in a riverscape when appropriate, such as the stern of the boat Jane No. 6 in *The Pool* (CHECKLIST 13), but tended to save them for interior and figural scenes. *Longshoremen* (CHECKLIST 15) has denser networks of shadow beneath the table, and on the planking of the table and walls. The figures still seem awkward, with expressions that only sometimes find their mark; Whistler would develop his talents in independent plates of the human figure represented outside of the sets contained in the MMFA collections.

Rotherhithe (CAT. ENTRY 6, P. 37), dated 1860, is one of the most accomplished of the etchings in the series and was originally issued as *Wapping*. It is closely related to the painting *Wapping* of 1860–64 (National Gallery of Art, Washington, D.C.). In the etching, Whistler carefully controlled the contrasts of the deeply bitten wood of the planks above each figure with the open view seen through the center of the plate. The line work in the rigging is masterful and assured, and the figures engage one another more naturally than in *Longshoremen*. The radical cropping of the midlength figures provides an early indication of Whistler's interest in Japanese color woodblock prints and their aesthetics. The one portrait print in the set, the drypoint *Becquet* (CAT. ENTRY 4, P. 31), seems a throwback to Rembrandt's early etchings in the sketchiness of both the background and the shadows on the face.

The Thames Set as a whole represents Whistler's first well-composed, mature set of prints. The series also suggests the variety of sources that the young artist was absorbing, from the old master prints of Rembrandt to the influence of contemporaries such as Meryon and Haden to the exotic formal elements of Japanese design. Only one of the prints is contemporary with the publication of the set in 1871: *Chelsea Bridge and Church* (CHECKLIST 29)—small, hastily done, and lightly bitten, qualities that make it stand in sharp contrast to the rest of the set.

Whistler had moved to Chelsea in 1863 and lived there, with rare breaks in Paris and Venice, for the rest of his life. Though many of the paintings of the 1860s reflect these new surroundings, the artist largely abandoned etching during the second half of the 1860s. Nonetheless he remained pleased with the etchings of the early French and Thames Sets, as they constituted a significant percentage of the twenty-four prints he exhibited in the Paris Universal Exposition of 1867.

Whistler worked episodically on etching and drypoint through the 1870s, preoccupied as he was with painting. The series of portraits that include his mother Anna Matilda McNeill Whistler, Cicely Alexander, Thomas Carlisle, and members of the Leyland family, advanced his reputation as a portraitist during this decade. His development of the nocturne as an approach to landscape parallels his portrait painting, establishing him as a pioneering champion and prophet of the overwhelming importance of formal elements in art. The MMFA collection includes three etchings and three lithographs that date from between the publication of the Thames Set and the trip to Venice. While each of the intaglios is an accomplished print, it is the lithographs that mark the progression in Whistler's development toward an art of ever increasing tonal subtlety.

Battersea: Dawn of 1875 (CHECKLIST 30) is a silvery, minimal drypoint cityscape of the far bank of the Thames as an island dominated by the river below and the expansive sky above. It has an air of insubstantiality that later appears in the most delicate of the Venice prints. The impression of the first state in the MMFA collection has a noble history, having been owned by the Royal Library at Windsor Palace and later by eminent Whistler collector and cataloguer Howard Mansfield. From 1878, *St. James's Street* (CAT. ENTRY 8, P. 43) presents a marvelous view rendered from an upper story window, reminiscent of the urban impressionist views of Whistler's colleagues Monet and Pissarro. In the MMFA's striking impression, a viewer can discern Whistler's use of only a bit of crosshatching in the foreground carriages to set off a rich contrast with the sunlight playing across the street. It is easy to forget Whistler's passion for detail in light of his goals in painting, but his etchings present vivid data on everyday life, such as this example which includes over seventy people. Whistler executed *The "Adam and Eve," Old Chelsea* (CAT. ENTRY 9, P. 47), the following year. In this case he may have utilized a photograph as an aid.[13] However, he carefully reversed the design of the image onto the plate so that it would be correctly oriented in the reversal of the printing process, something he did not always take the effort to do.

The lithographs Whistler executed in 1878 are far more atmospheric than anything he had yet attempted in etching and drypoint. This had to do with the expressive vocabulary inherent in the lithographic process, one that allowed the artist to conceive and work the design in tone rather than line. Thomas Way, the printer who taught Whistler lithography, arranged for Whistler to draw and paint on a stone while floating on a barge on the Thames in the dock area of East London where Whistler had first etched twenty years before.[14] For *Limehouse* (CHECKLIST 56) the artist worked with a half-tinted stone, darkening some areas and scraping others to lighten the inking, creating a far more atmospheric image than he had previously done in any print technique. On *Nocturne* (CAT. ENTRY 24, P. 85) Whistler achieved a more subtle treatment of light playing across the river and the far shore of Battersea at dusk. *Nocturne* clearly foreshadows the work Whistler would create in Venice, leaving some question as to why the astute artist never turned to lithography in rendering that most atmospheric of cities.

The story of Whistler in Venice is the centerpiece to the Whistler legend, a tale of fall from grace, exile, and triumphant return. The narrative begins with the Whistler-Ruskin trial of 1878, and concludes with two exhibitions at the commercial Fine Art Society in 1880–81. In the late 1870s Whistler's reputation for pugnaciousness reached its apogee with the artist's well-publicized libel suit against the eminent Victorian art critic John Ruskin. The events leading up to the trial began with a review by Ruskin that appeared in July 1877 issue of his *Fors Clavigera*, the now-famous condemnation of Whistler's work in an exhibition at Sir Coutts Lindsay's new Grosvenor Gallery:

> For Mr. Whistler's own sake, no less than for the protection of the purchaser, Sir Coutts Lindsay ought not to have admitted works into the gallery in which the ill-educated conceit of the artist so nearly approached the aspect of wilful imposture. I have seen, and heard, much of Cockney impudence before now; but never expected to hear a coxcomb ask two hundred guineas for flinging a pot of paint in the public's face.[15]

Whistler made a calculated decision to bring suit against the critic for libel, resulting in perhaps the most celebrated trial in the history of art, Whistler v. Ruskin. The initial action in the suit took place in August 1877, with Whistler's attorney notifying Ruskin of his client's intention to seek damages for libel. Pretrial motions, and frequent postponements due to Ruskin's ill health, delayed the proceedings until November 25, 1878. The trial focused attention on the artistic debates of the day and provided many memorable and sometimes humorous, exchanges between Whistler and the defense attorney.[16] Despite the series of delays that led up to the trial, the actual presentation of the case took only eight hours, and the jurors needed only a couple of hours the following day to reach a conclusion. They found in favor of Whistler, agreeing that Ruskin had committed libel, but awarded him only one farthing (a quarter of a penny), rather than the £1,000 that he had sought in the action. Interpreting the jury's award as a strong reproach to Whistler for having brought the matter to trial, the judge directed that the two sides each absorb their own expenses. The decision led to Whistler's bankruptcy in May 1879, a substantial price to pay for a largely symbolic victory. By the summer financial insolvency and a lack of new patronage resulting from adverse publicity left Whistler reeling; he accepted a commission from a commercial gallery in London, the Fine Art Society, to etch a series of prints of Venice for December holiday sales.

In September, Whistler departed for Venice with the intention of producing twelve etchings over a period of three months. In the end, the artist remained in Venice for fourteen months, during which he executed more than fifty prints, a handful of paintings, and approximately one hundred pastels. The etchings are at the core of Whistler's Venetian achievement. Upon his return to England, the exhibitions of his Venetian etchings and pastels reestablished his artistic reputation, and provided a turning point in his career.

Whistler's stylistic innovations, as well as the influence of his vision on subsequent generations of printmakers, are embodied in the two Venice Sets. The MMFA owns ten of the twelve prints from the First Venice Set, missing only the *Little Lagoon* and the *Palaces*. Only eight of the twenty-six prints in the Second Venice Set are in the collection, but the relative paucity of representation in this series is compensated by the fine quality of these particular impressions.

Whistler arrived in Venice late in September, and although he had agreed to finish the plates by December, it soon became clear that he would miss his deadline. During the unusually cold autumn and winter of 1879–80 Whistler suffered, as Venice lacked the modern conveniences of London. In an early letter to his sister-in-law Helen Whistler, he lamented how he missed London and complained about the Italian language, the Venetian food, and how the cold was limiting his progress on the commission.[17] Subsequently he wrestled with the subject matter of Venice, overwhelmed by the remarkable visual riches of the city. He wanted to develop his own approach to the city, one that would distinguish his work from the anecdotal sentimentality of established Victorian imagery. His achievement relied in part on this original conception of a Venice that was best known to contemporary Venetians—the long vistas, the back alleys, the quiet canals and idiosyncratic bridges that cross them, and the isolated squares of the everyday life of the city.

In his etchings Whistler generally eschewed certain subjects: landmarks of architecture, interiors, and large-scale figural scenes. The artist rendered few images of the usual sights, the Piazza San Marco, the Basilica, and the Grand Canal. Occasionally Whistler did record a notable site, as in the etching *The Piazzetta* (CAT. ENTRY 13, P. 57). In this case, as in all of the Venice prints, Whistler drew the image directly on a prepared etching plate allowing the normal reversal of the printing process to render the scene in mirror image. He claimed that his intent was not to produce picturesque and recognizable scenes for the British tourist, but to produce etched masterpieces of design and tone.[18] Whistler's refusal to reverse his Venetian images on the plate often is mentioned as one of the artist's innovations, yet a number of previously un-cited precedents exist: Canaletto's 1744 etching *The Marketplace on the Molo* clearly shows the church and island of San Giorgio Maggiore in reverse in the back ground; eighteenth-century optical views sometimes reversed their images; and Adolphe Appian's 1878 etching *Boats at Anchor, Venice* represents the church of Santa Maria della Salute and the customs house in mirror image.[19]

Throughout his career, Whistler was not above a calculated bit of misdirection in suggesting the reasons for his aesthetic decisions. While it is true that his direct work on a plate resulted in a mirror image of the site, other possible explanations exist for his rationale in this working method. He had come of age with a generation of artists in France, primarily the impressionists, who valued the informality and spontaneity garnered in the process of drawing and painting in the presence of the motif. Imagine the laboriousness for Whistler had he needed first to execute a careful drawing of a site, only to have to either trace it, or reproduce it freehand, upon the plate. The process would have robbed the plate of all of the immediacy Whistler hoped to capture in rendering the scene. Mortimer Menpes, Joseph Pennell, Otto Bacher, and other post-Whistlerian artists such as Ernest David Roth and John Marin understood this and employed the same idea for their prints of Venice. Unlike Whistler and many of his followers, Scottish artist James McBey believed that the etched view should be seen with the natural orientation of the subject, so that the plate initially should be drawn in reverse. McBey turned his back on the scene he was recording and drew his image looking into a rear view automobile mirror that he had mounted on his easel.[20]

One of the singular characteristics of Whistler's Venetian etchings is the painstaking development of a key motif, the focal point of a design that expands out from the center of the image but not to the limits of the sheet. His predilection for detailing only the important elements of the design, leaving the marginal and other ancillary areas incomplete, is part of the avant-garde nature of his art. The etching *The Doorway* (CAT. ENTRY 12, P. 55) is an example of this approach. The artist added a film of ink to the lower portion of this plate prior to printing, to indicate the murkiness of the water in contrast to the precise delineation of the palace. Whistler either printed each impression himself or supervised the printing so that each of the images that utilize selective wiping is unique. His preference for images of contemporary Venice combined with his avant-garde compositional structure and his novelty in inking produced works of startling modernity.

Almost half of Whistler's prints are panoramas, distant vistas across or along an expanse of water, of the skyline of Venice and the lagoon islands. Whistler tended to position these views on horizontal sheets, exploiting the sense of distance through a broad horizon, as in *Little Venice* (CHECKLIST 33) where the format reinforces the suggestion of a spacious view. Whistler demonstrated a refined sensibility by matching his images with the appropriate shapes and orientations of each sheet. As in *Doorway*, Whistler sometimes added additional surface tone to his prints by selectively wiping the copper plates, leaving a thin film of ink on parts of the image. When he printed these plates, the veils of ink suggested particular lighting conditions resulting from his observations of different times of day and atmospheric conditions on the same scene. These selectively wiped prints are, in this regard, responses that parallel the impressionist program for capturing a subject under specific and accurate lighting conditions. The richly inked *Nocturne* (CAT. ENTRY 10, P. 49) from the First Venice Set and *Nocturne: Palaces* (CHECKLIST 44) from the Second Venice Set, are the two outstanding examples of Whistler's tonal wiping in the collection of the MMFA. These two impressions convey the sometimes dramatic, sometimes subtle effects of illumination the artist achieved employing this technique.

One of Whistler's favorite Venetian subjects was the close-up of a palace fronting on a small canal, tightly cropped and seen straight on from across the water. Often he gave no visual indication of the size or structure of the remainder of the buildings. Instead, using vertical formats, he focused upon the inherent geometric shapes of the openings in the façades of the buildings and the decorative patterns of the surface. *The Balcony* (CAT. ENTRY 19, P. 73) from the Second Venice Set is one of the most beautifully composed and balanced of these subjects. Whistler's precision can be seen in his handling of the flat-bottomed sandolo (often mistaken for a gondola) moored at the palace on this cleanly wiped impression. In all Whistler's Venice etchings, the artist's graphic shorthand, indebted to his study of Rembrandt, adds to the freshness and sparkle of the city's palaces, canals and alleys.

In the printing of the two Venice sets, Whistler began cutting his sheets to the plate mark, leaving just a tab for his penciled butterfly signature and the letters "imp." denoting that he himself had printed the impression. He publicly maintained that British collectors put too great a stock in the amount of margin surrounding old master prints, extrapolating this to contemporary printmakers.[21] Other authors have suggested that the cost of rare and expensive papers forced this economy, or that the plates themselves often cut through the paper at the plate mark, and that Whistler made a virtue of these necessities. Another possible rationale, however, is equally plausible. The layers of surface inking on many of the etchings likely left the plates difficult to handle in moving the inked plate to the bed of the press and in the careful placement of the paper over the copper prior to printing. A proof could be pulled more expeditiously if the printer did not need to exercise as much precaution in the handling of the paper, trimming away any soiled borders after the printing.

Whistler left Venice in November 1880, returning to London where he immediately set about printing the twelve etchings for the Fine Art Society. The initial exhibition of the First Venice Set opened in the small back room of the commercial establishment on December 1, 1880. The show failed to achieve great financial success, although it received good coverage in the daily periodicals and art journals. While critics debated the merits of Whistler's etchings, his fellow artists quickly perceived and embraced the freshness of Whistler's vision.

Whistler continued to create prints of exquisite refinement during the next fifteen years, including nearly half of his intaglio oeuvre, however, the MMFA collection includes only a handful of prints executed after 1880. Among the most interesting is the *Grand' Place, Brussels* (CAT. ENTRY 23, P. 83) of 1887. The remarkable impression in the MMFA reveals Whistler pursuing a new direction in printmaking. He spent an enormous amount of energy capturing the details of windows and ornaments across the façade, clearly excited by the play of light that dissolves the substance of the monumental building. He kept surface tone to a minimum in the foreground of this brilliant impression, as it is in many of the editions.

On August 11, 1888, Whistler married Beatrice Godwin, the affluent widow of his friend and collaborator, architect E. W. Godwin. In September of the following year, Whistler and Trixie spent two months in Amsterdam where the artist drew ten plates that he hoped to publish as a set through the Fine Art Society. However, since he had never completed the editions of the First Venice Set of 1880, the firm declined his offer.[22] The MMFA has only *Long House—Dyer's—Amsterdam* (CHECKLIST 55) of 1889, from the presumptive Amsterdam Set. The etching represents the style of the last phase of Whistler's career, extensive networks of fine lines have replaced the economy so characteristic of the earlier Venice sets. In the Amsterdam series, Whistler creates his tones entirely in deeply bitten and densely drawn lines, obviating the need for the selective wiping for tonal effects needed in the laborious printing of the Venice nocturnes. Whistler believed the set to be the synthesis of the virtues of his earliest style in the Thames Set and the compositional advances of the Venice sets. In an article of March 11, 1890, in the *Pall Mall Budget*, he is recorded as having first displayed and discussed the individual Amsterdam etchings, and then to have summed up his etching career in this way:

> "I divide myself into three periods," he says, being in his most serious and sensible mood. "First you see me at work on the Thames," producing one of the famous series. "Now, there you have the crude and hard detail of the beginner. So far, so good. There, you see, all is sacrificed to exactitude of outline. Presently, and almost unconsciously, I begin to criticize myself, and to feel the craving of the artist for form and colour. The result was the second stage, which my enemies call The Inchoate, and I call Impressionism. The third stage I have shown you. In that I have endeavoured to combine stages one and two. You have the elaboration of the first stage and the quality of the second."[23]

Whistler's early etchings from the French Set show his youthful enthusiasm for detail with the horror vacui of the novice. Their achievements in composition lead to the greater confidence and economy of line that Whistler achieved in the Thames Set, mostly drawn within two years of the first set. The two Venice sets reveal his reduction of design to an ever greater extent, while compensating for the more minimal line work with the exquisite inking that defines the atmosphere of the exotic lagoon city. The late Amsterdam work returns to the heavily worked passages of his youthful series, but with the mature sense of composition and design learned over an extended experimentation with the medium. The history of Whistler's development is read and appreciated through his advances in the application of tonal elements, most evident in the extended examination of his accomplishments in the sets of prints he conceived throughout his career as a printmaker.

TECHNICAL DISCUSSION

A discussion of the technical aspects of etching helps place Whistler in the context of the developing vocabulary of printmaking in the nineteenth century. Etching, which goes back to the first years of the sixteenth century, may be seen as a variation of the technique of engraving. Both are in the family of intaglio printmaking, defined by the incising of lines and shapes to form a design on a metal plate. In engraving the design is cut with a burin that physically removes a strip of metal from the plate. A variant of engraving is drypoint, where a sharp, hard point is dragged through the metal surface, creating a scratch that has a delicate area of furrow of metal on the side of the line, or burr, which gives the line a soft velvety appearance while it briefly lasts prior to wearing during inking and printing. In etching and its associated tonal process of aquatint, the design is created not by manually removing metal, but by coating the copper surface with an acid-resistant layer, and then drawing through that layer to expose the plate to acid. After allowing the acid to "bite" into the plate, the protective layer is removed revealing a surface with a similar incised design to the engraving. A thick, viscous ink is applied to the surface and forced into the grooves of the plate. Traditionally, the surface is wiped clean to allow the white of the paper to form a contrast to the dark lines of the composition. An artist may elect to leave a film of ink across the surface, adding tonal variations to the paper, or even to paint motifs on the surface of the plate that add to the composition but may only be printed once. Whistler selectively wiped images throughout most of his career. ***Eric Denker***

ENDNOTES

1. For example, see Robert Rosenblum and H. W. Janson, *19th-Century Art* (New York: Harry N. Abrams, 1984), and Petra Ten-Doesschate Chu, *Nineteenth-Century European Art* (New York: Harry N. Abrams, 2003).
2. Anonymous author, in conversation with James McNeill Whistler, "The Red Rag," *The World* (London), May 22, 1878, as quoted by Thorp, *Whistler on Art*, pp. 51–52.
3. John Godfrey Saxe, *The Blind Men and the Elephant* (New York: McGraw-Hill, 1963).
4. Nicolai Cikovsky, Jr., with Charles Brock, "Whistler and America," in Dorment and MacDonald, *James McNeill Whistler*, pp. 29–38.
5. Saxe, *Blind Men*.
6. Charles Baudelaire, "Painters and Etchers," *Le Boulevard (Paris)*, September 14, 1862, as quoted in Spencer, *Whistler*, p. 60.
7. Denker, *In Pursuit of the Butterfly*. This volume also serves as a brief biography of the artist as illustrated through the portraits of the artist by Whistler and his contemporaries.
8. John Ross Key, "Recollections of Whistler while in the Office of the United States Coast Survey," *Century Magazine*, April 1908, as quoted in Spencer, *Whistler*, p. 53.
9. Illustrated in the standard catalogue raisonné of Whistler's prints: Kennedy, *Etched Work of Whistler*, no. 27. Whistler's friend and colleague Henri Fantin-Latour copied the *Veronese Marriage Feast at Cana*, a version of which Haden had purchased in 1859. Pennell & Pennell, *Life of Whistler*, p. 77.
10. Reproduced in Kennedy, *Etched Work of Whistler*, p. xl.
11. Frederick Wedmore, "Mr. Whistler's Etching," *Saturday Review*, August 12, 1871, as cited in Spencer, *Whistler*, p. 95.
12. Francis Seymour Haden, *Yacht Tavern, Erith*, 1865, etching on zinc; Maxime Lalanne, *Demolition for the Opening of the rue des Ecoles* (*Demolitions pour le percement de la rue des Ecoles)*, ca. 1862, etching; Maxime Lalanne, *Demolitions pour le percement du boulevard Saint-Germain*, ca. 1862, etching, exhibited in *Prints by Whistler and His Contemporaries*, p. 5; all in the collection of the National Gallery of Art, Washington, D.C.
13. Nigel Thorp, "Studies in Black and White: Whistler's Photographs in Glasgow University Library," in Ruth E. Fine, ed., *James McNeill Whistler: A Reevaluation, Studies in the History of Art*, vol. 17 (Washington D.C.: National Gallery of Art, 1987), pp. 96–98.
14. Tedeschi et al., *Lithographs of James McNeill Whistler*, pp. 58–62.
15. John Ruskin, "Letter 79: Life Guards of New Life," *Fors Clavigera* 7 (July 1877), as collected in E.T. Cook and Alexander Wedderburn, eds., *The Works of John Ruskin* (London: George Allen, 1903–12), vol. 29, p. 160.
16. Merrill, *Pot of Paint*, pp. 59–71. Merrill has painstakingly reconstructed the arguments from various sources to produce the most complete account of the trial now possible.
17. Letters reproduced in MacDonald, *Palaces in the Night*, pp. 141–45.
18. Walter Sickert later complained about the reversal of the images, wishing them reproduced in reverse for those who were familiar with the actual locations. Walter Sickert, "The New Life of Whistler," *Fortnightly Review*, December 1908, as cited in Robins, *Walter Sickert*, p. 182.
19. Whistler may have known Appian's etching, which was published in the print journal *L'eau-forte* in Paris in 1879.
20. Martin Hardie, "The Etched Work of James McBey," *Print Collector's Quarterly 25* (1938): 427 as cited in Denker, *Whistler and His Circle in Venice*, p. 45.
21. Lochnan, *Etchings of James McNeill Whistler*, p. 212. Lochnan's book is the best examination of Whistler's career as a printmaker and the starting point for any scholar commencing a Whistler print project.
22. Lochnan, *Etchings of James McNeill Whistler* p. 253.
23. Anonymous author, "A Chat with Mr. Whistler," *Pall Mall Budget*, March 13, 1890, as reproduced in Spencer, *Whistler*, pp. 269–70.

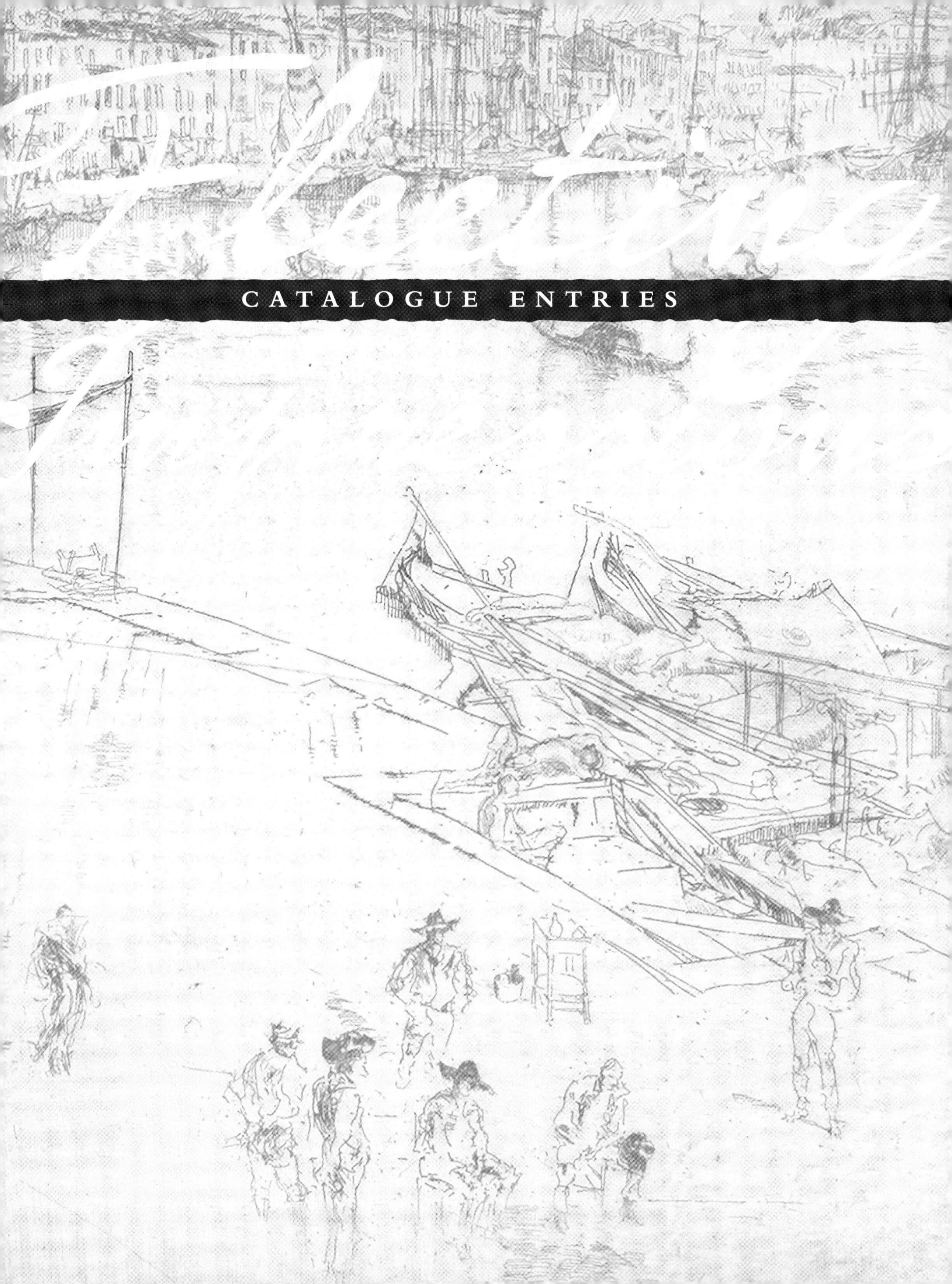

CATALOGUE ENTRIES

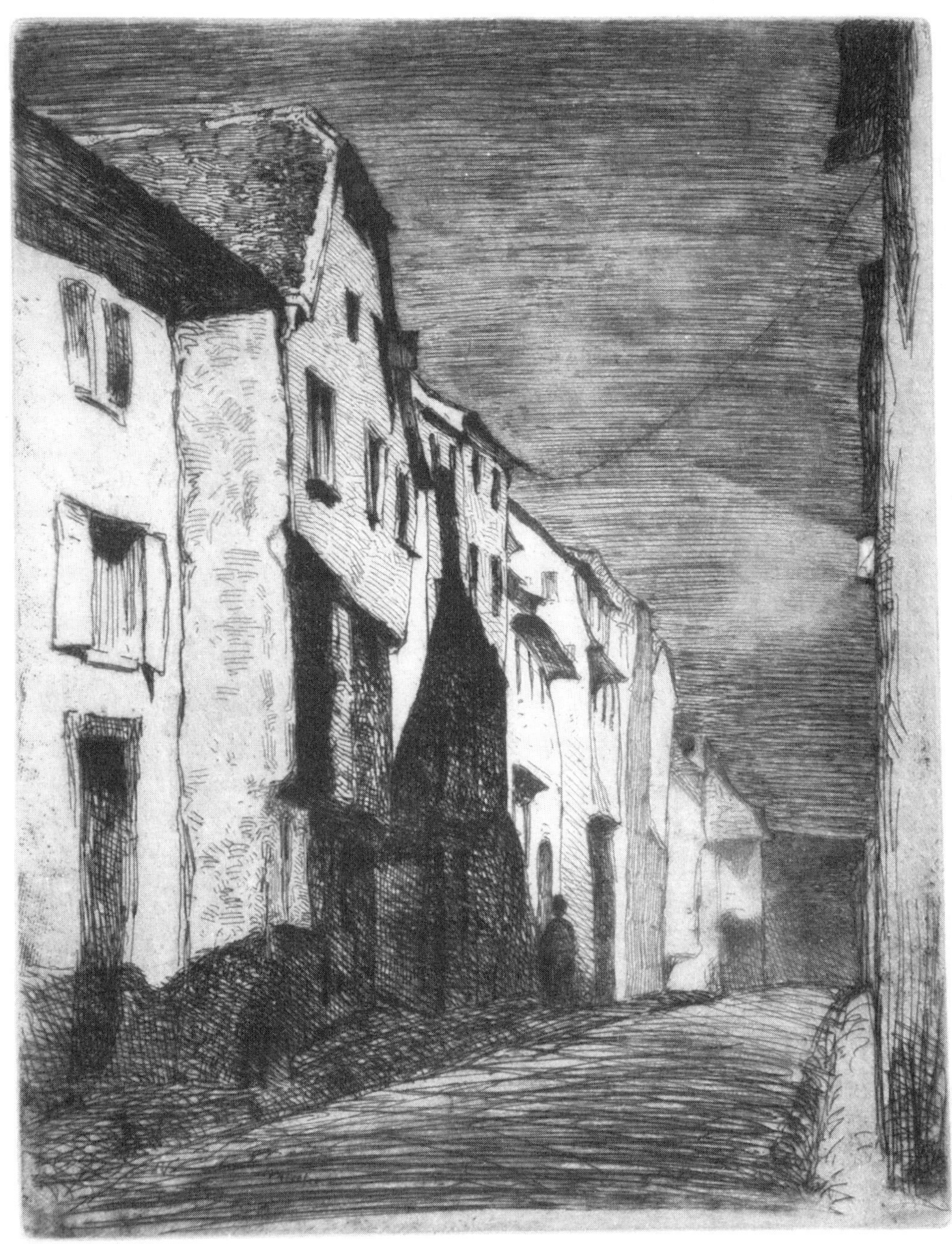

One of "Twelve Etchings from Nature" (French Set)
Etching
Japanese paper
Signed, recto, lower left on plate: "Whistler"
Kennedy 19 v/V; Mansfield 19
Checklist 2

Street at Saverne, 1858

CATALOGUE ENTRY 1

Street at Saverne is one of "Twelve Etchings from Nature," generally referred to as the French Set, that became the initial landmark of Whistler's early career as a printmaker and placed him among the avant-garde artists of the burgeoning etching revival in Paris. All twelve are based upon Whistler's journey through eastern France and western Germany during the late summer and early autumn of 1858. *Street at Saverne* was drawn and etched on the journey and is the first for which a preparatory drawing survives.[1] Except for a few economical changes, the etched image is faithful to the sketch.

The print is noteworthy for several reasons: it is Whistler's initial attempt to depict a nocturnal setting; it is the artist's first etching to represent a street scene; and it demonstrates Whistler's growing interest in contrasting effect of light and shadow, chiaroscuro. The strong lines and rich tones of the image recall the solidity of etchings by Rembrandt, the Dutch master Whistler most admired and wished to emulate.

Whistler depicted an empty street scene with very few visual clues. He rendered the street receding into the distance, flanked by a row of buildings. The upper floors of the buildings, probably residences, jut out over the street, creating an almost tunnel-like composition. The dark printing of the image, along with the slightly claustrophobic feeling created by the architecture, lends an ominous tone to the scene. The lantern on the façade of a building on the right side casts a dramatic shadow on the buildings on the left side of the street. The shadow deepens the somber mood. As the buildings recede into the distance, the details of the architecture become faint amorphous masses, an apparition of undefined structures.

Street at Saverne was intended as a nocturnal scene using "artistic printing," a highly charged contemporary phrase during the etching revival. Artistic printing was the deliberate application of ink to the surface of the plate to obtain tonal effects, meaning that the resulting impression was composed of more than just the etched lines on the plate. In the 1850s many artists decried this practice, claiming that the technique lay outside of the boundaries of true etching. Many other artists, however, were intrigued by the aesthetic possibilities, including Auguste Delâtre, the printer who produced the French Set and who, along with Francis Seymour Haden, introduced Whistler to a variety of approaches to printing.

The MMFA's impression of *Street at Saverne* lacks Delâtre's name and address. That change occurred when Whistler printed the fifth and final state, soon after his return from Venice in 1880, and created an image that is much darker than the earlier ones.[2] The artist incorporated his greater expertise in printing, including the extremely nuanced application of plate tone to each impression, to achieve more delicate transitions than in the earlier states. Whistler shifted the visual focus in the ultimate state, emphasizing the lantern and further enhancing the wide range of tones employed in the image. EKJ

1. Lochnan "Whistler's Etchings," p. 79.
2. MacNamara & Siewart, *Prosaic Views, Poetic Vision*, p. 37.

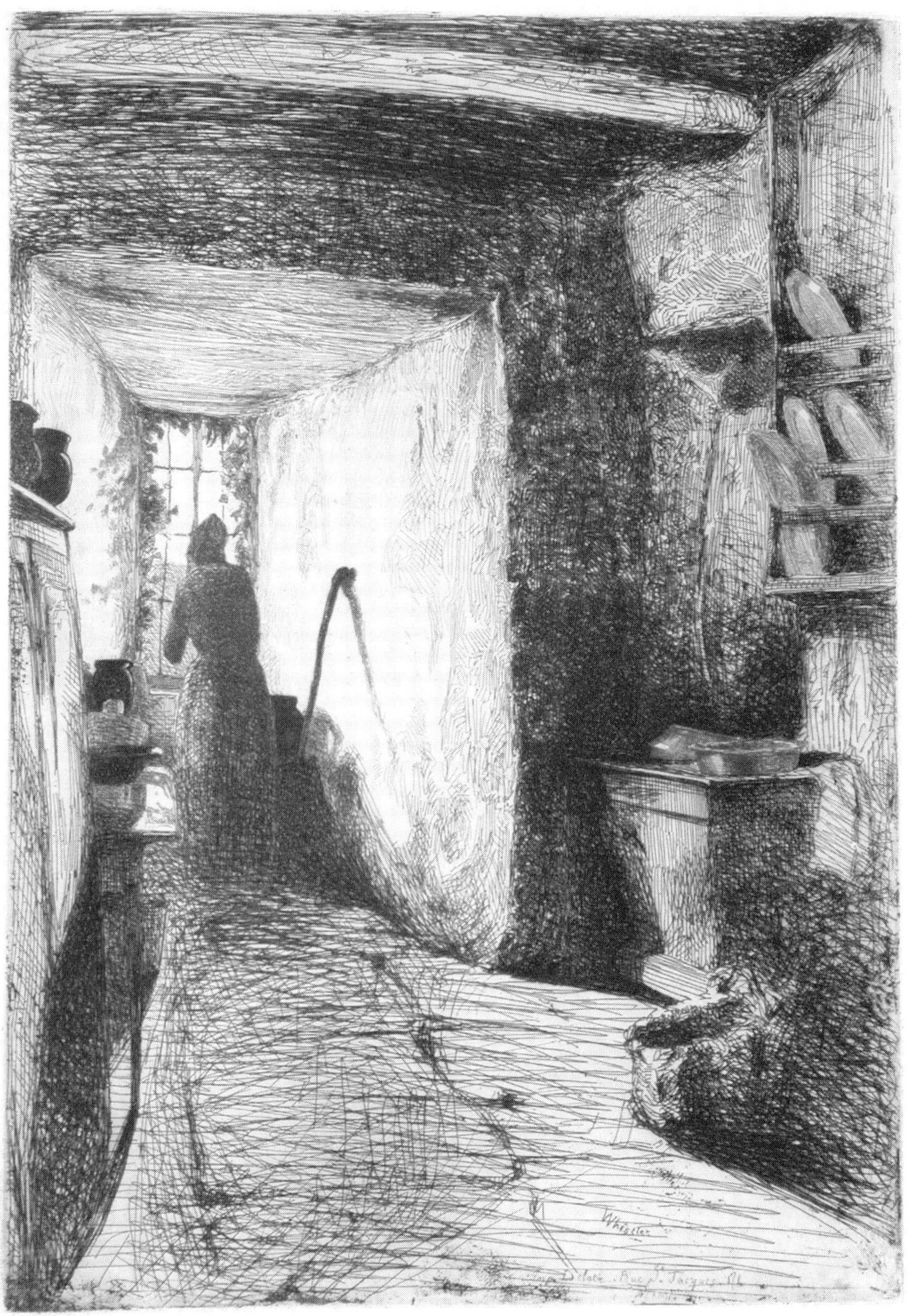

One of "Twelve Etchings from Nature" (French Set)
Etching
Wove paper
Signed, recto, lower right on plate: "Whistler"
Kennedy 24 ii/III; Mansfield 24
Checklist 4

The Kitchen, 1858

Critics in the middle of the nineteenth century and many scholars today consider *The Kitchen* one of the most powerful of Whistler's early images. The print remained in such high esteem that the owners of the plate, the Fine Art Society of London, produced fifty additional impressions for sale in 1884–85.[1] Unlike the early impression in the MMFA, those later states include Whistler's butterfly signature on a small tab on the lower side of the print and significant plate tone, an artistic technique that Whistler employed more regularly in his later etchings.

Whistler made both a pencil drawing and a watercolor sketch of the scene while in Lutzelbourg, a village very close to Saverne, the site of *Street at Saverne* (CAT. ENTRY 1, P. 25), but according to Francis Seymour Haden, Whistler's brother-in-law and etching companion, the artist completed the final composition only after his return to Paris. The etching bears an almost exact correspondence to the watercolor: a single figure in front of a window in an interior domestic space.[2] Whistler used the watercolor to explore the effects of differing tonal values within the composition.

Whistler's etching evoked many artistic references important to mid-nineteenth-century viewers, which may explain part of its popularity. The subject matter and the pose of the female figure resemble that in *La Cuisinière*, a painting Whistler's close friend and artistic companion François Bonvin had displayed at the 1849 Salon. The paintings of Pieter de Hooch likely influenced Whistler's choice of a tranquil domestic interior scene in which the intimacy of doorways and windows frame the subject. The figure that fades into deep shadows as well as the lighting of the composition, a space illuminated from within, convey the impact of Rembrandt's designs on the young artist.[3]

Yet, *The Kitchen* offers more than simply a youthful composite of references. Whistler drew on these influences but then synthesized and developed them into his own artistic vision. He ambitiously employed the capacity of etching to express contrasts of light and dark tones in the alternating, receding spaces of the room as it unfolds before the viewer. The distinctive patterning of the floor anticipates the emphasis on pattern that came to shape Whistler's vision, both in printmaking and in painting. The figure of the woman emerges from the strong patterning in the shadowy area of the window niche. The bright light streams through the window into the dark interior, suggesting the sensation of looking into space through a porthole. The effect for the viewers is voyeuristic, looking into a quiet, contained world that refrains from acknowledging our presence in the composition. In *The Kitchen* Whistler combined a respect for tradition and the Old Masters with a novel appreciation of the tonal possibilities of etching, resulting in Whistler's first, great etching masterpiece.[4] EKJ

1. MacNamara & Siewart, *Prosaic Views, Poetic Vision*, p. 41.
2. Lochnan "Whistler's Etchings," p. 80.
3. Ibid., p. 86.
4. Ibid., p. 87.

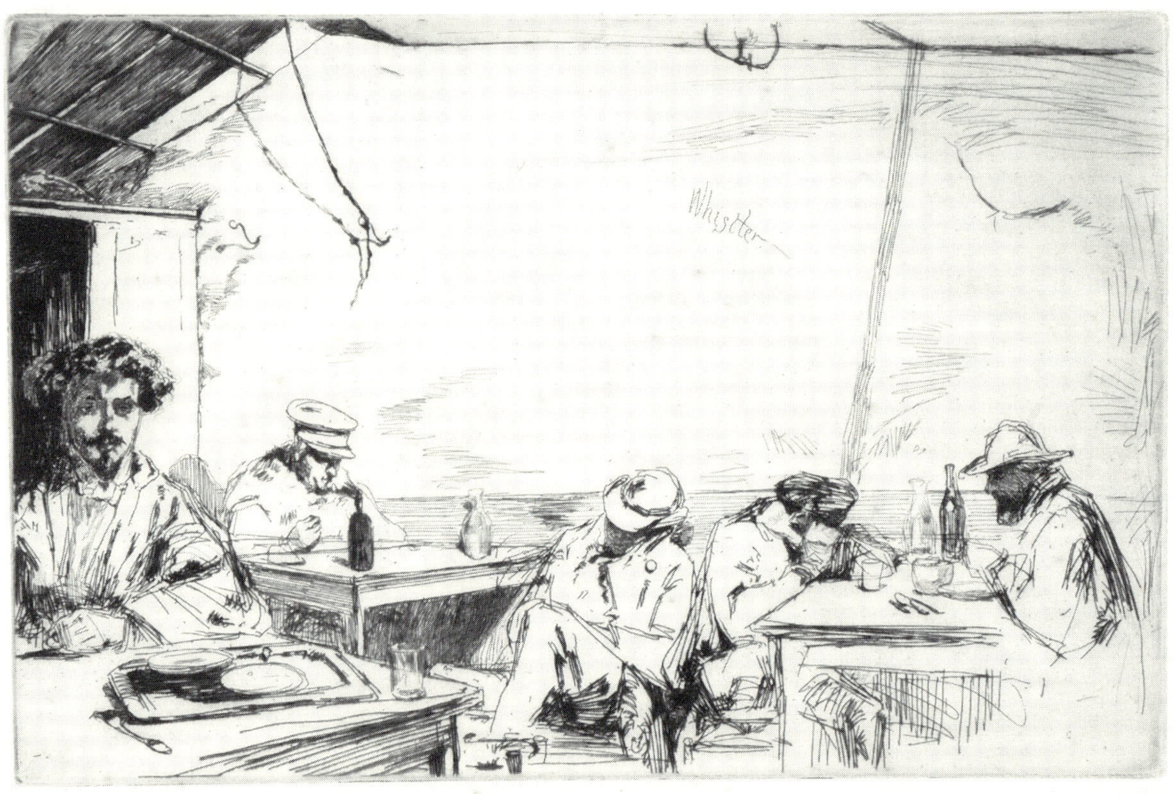

Drypoint
Japanese paper
Signed, recto, upper right in plate: "Whistler"
Kennedy 49, only state; Mansfield 49
Checklist 18

Soupe à Trois Sous, 1859

CATALOGUE ENTRY 3

Whistler created *Soupe à Trois Sous* in Paris in late 1859 as an experiment with the technique of drypoint, a form of intaglio printmaking that largely had fallen into disuse after Rembrandt's era. Unlike etching, in which acid creates the incisions on a plate, drypoint involves drawing with a steel or diamond point directly onto a bare, ungrounded, metal surface, most often copper. Therefore, drypoint is a more direct technique than etching, requiring fewer steps between the artist's drawing on the plate and the production of the image. An early impression of a drypoint image is characterized by a soft, velvety line with a feathery burr, the term for the adjacent copper shards displaced by the needle. Drypoint images are extremely delicate, yielding only a few impressions before the lines lose their richness, and the painterly effects for which the medium is so highly valued.

Whistler's brother-in-law Francis Seymour Haden owned a fine collection of Rembrandt drypoints, and these exerted a powerful influence on the young artist. Whistler created this etching soon after arriving in London from Paris, and both in style and subject matter it parallels his Thames Set etchings, mostly executed in 1859–60. The plate reflects Whistler's interest in an exploration of low-life subjects, employing a "radical elimination of detail, the naïve style of drawing" and the construction of the pictorial space in a receding series of planes that developed in the London etchings.[1]

The scene depicts a lower-class eatery that late into the night offered soup for 3 sous, a very inexpensive meal. The expanse of blank wall dominating the center weighs down the figures dispersed along the lower register of the composition. Whistler conveyed the fatigue among the tired workers by their poses and postures: hunched figures lean wearily over the table. Most of them are anonymous, their expressions hidden, with the exception of a single young man who peers out of the composition and directly engages the viewer. The deeply inked lines of his face and hair make the painterly, soft characteristics of the drypoint clearly evident in the MMFA's rich impression.

Despite Whistler's initial interest in the visual effects of drypoint, he did not immediately pursue his exploration of this technique, although many later prints relied on drypoint to augment the atmospheric effects of the traditional etching method. Yet, Whistler's early use of drypoint proved important within the context of his career as a printmaker. His attraction to atmospheric effects that are achieved through soft lines and subtle tone persisted throughout Whistler's career, in paintings, as well as in later works on paper. Possibly Whistler did not find the medium of drypoint, with its limited printing capabilities and delicacy of surface, practical during the period in which he strove to establish his reputation as a printmaker and distribute his works to a wider audience. EKJ

1. Lochnan, "Whistler's Etchings," p. 140.

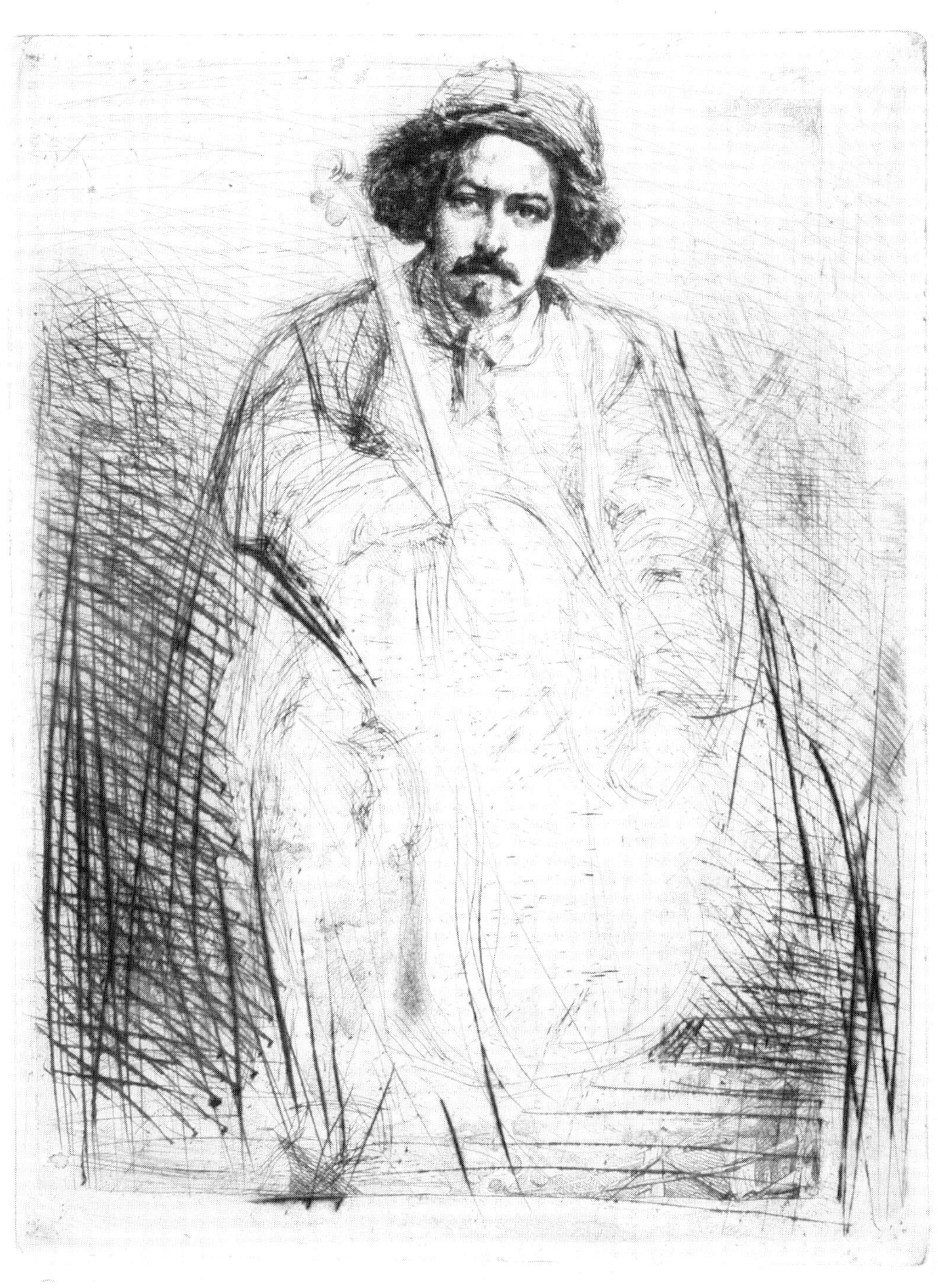

One of "Sixteen Etchings of Scenes of the Thames" (Thames Set)
Drypoint
Laid paper
Kennedy 52 iii/IV; Mansfield 52
Checklist 19

Becquet, 1859

CATALOGUE ENTRY 4

Whistler's early etched work reveals a wide variety of approaches and artistic influences. He first experimented with printmaking while a cadet at West Point, evidence of which survives in *Becquet*. He had initially used the plate to depict a scene of the Military Academy while there as a student, 1851–54, and remnants of that original design exist in the lower right corner: a faint detail of stacked muskets. Throughout his career Whistler reused copper etching plates by scraping off the earlier images, but this lively portrait of friend and fellow artist, sculptor Just Becquet, alone retains the ghost of the earlier print.

Becquet is also an interesting early example of Whistler's experimentation with drypoint. The marks left on the plate by the diamond-tip needle range from shallow to deep, and both left copper debris (burr) on either side of the furrows. Whistler liked these effects, and later explained:

> The tiny thread of metal ploughed out of the line by the point as it runs along, clings to its edge through its whole length and, in the printing, holds the ink in a clogged manner, and produces, in the proof, a soft velvety effect most painter like and beautiful—and precious too, for this raised edge soon falls off the plate, from the continued wiping in printing—so that early proofs only have the velvety line and are also, because of its presence, valued... In an etching there is no "burr" as such ridge of the metal is immediately dissolved by the acid and the line is left clean. The impression is consequently quite crisp and without soft velvet effect of the drypoint "burr."[1]

Whistler executed this image with powerful dark drypoint lines that hold the dense ink. He varied the intensity of the lines, emphasizing the contours of the sitter's face and shoulders. Striving to capture the essential elements of sculptor Becquet's personality in the print he depicted this amateur musician looking directly at the viewer in a confident but compassionate manner. He skillfully manipulated the lines, outlining the arms to suggest movement and the sounds of music, yet provided no specific indication or proof that Becquet is playing the instrument. According to Whistler biographers Joseph and Elizabeth Pennell, Becquet lived "in his [Paris] studio where there was nothing but disorder and his cello."[2] Although "the greatest man who ever lived to his friends," such as Whistler who met him while a student in Paris, Becquet remained "to the world unknown."[3]

Whistler changed the title of the image to *The Fiddler* and included the portrait in his 1871 Thames Set, making it one of only two etchings in the set that did not depict the River Thames. Although a portrait and not a riverscape, the print articulated Whistler's new approach to pictorial construction that defined the aesthetics of the Thames Set. The harsh lines of the drypoint technique emphasized his interest in manipulating perspectives and focus within a picture plane. The amount of detail in the figure's face markedly contrasted with the loose outline of his body, and the informality of the latter suggested movement, music, and life. JWR

1. Whistler to Charles Sissler, n.d., Rosenwald Collection, National Gallery of Art, Washington, D.C.
2. Pennell & Pennell, *Whistler Journal*, p. 90.
3. Pennell & Pennell, *Life of Whistler* (1914 ed.), p. 49. See also, A. Estignard, *Just Becquet* (Besançon: De la Maison Delagrange, 1911), p. 3.

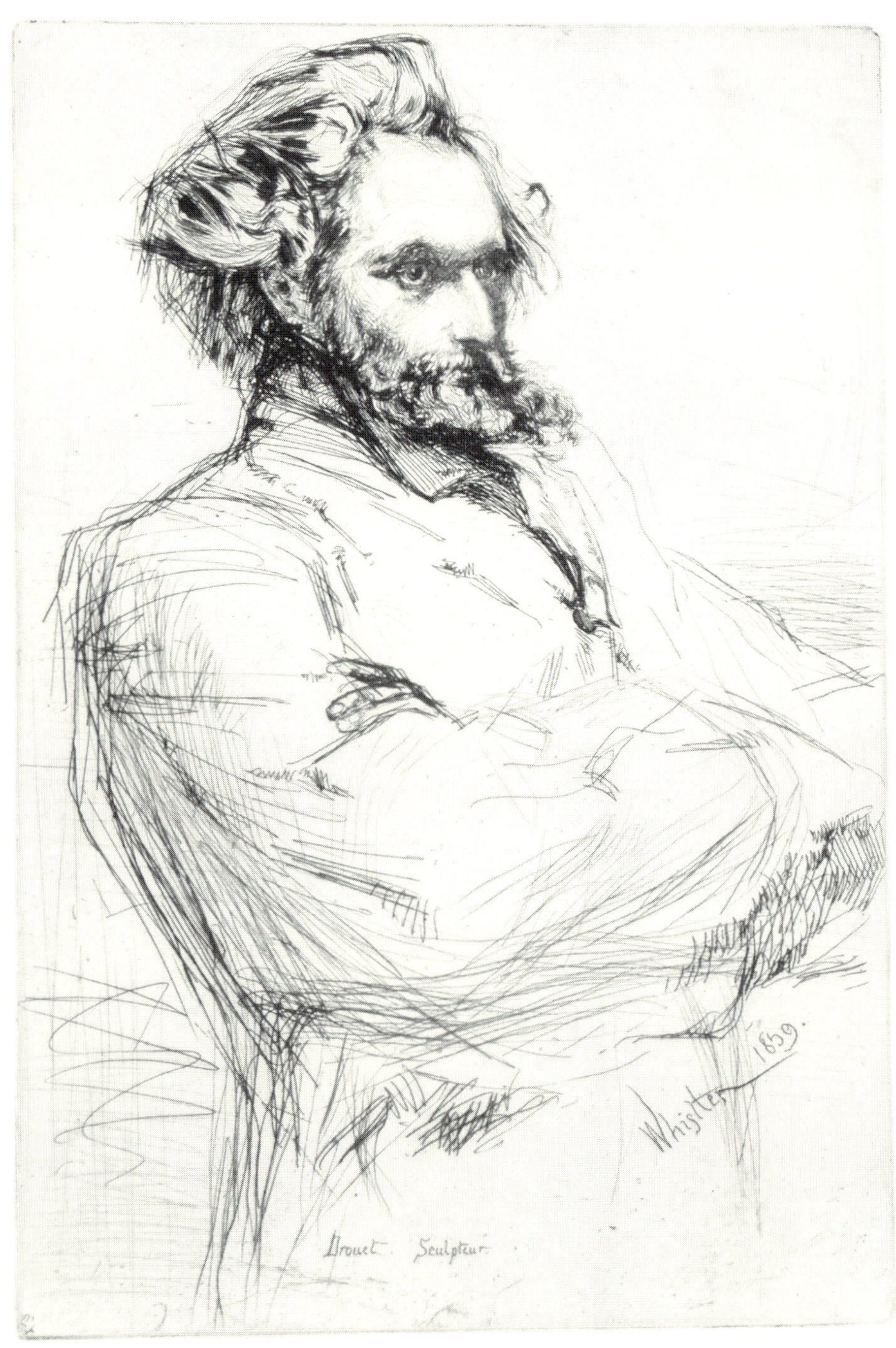

Drypoint
Japanese paper
Signed, recto, lower right in plate:
"Whistler 1859"
Kennedy 55 ii/II; Mansfield 55
Checklist 20

Drouet, 1859

As a young art student in Paris during the mid 1850s, trying to define his own identity and style, Whistler familiarized himself with the avant-garde work of Barbizon landscapists and realist painters, particularly Gustave Courbet. When Whistler arrived in Paris, Courbet's revolutionary one-man exhibit was installed adjacent to the Universal Exposition on Avenue Montaigne. In his realist manifesto of 1855, Courbet had declared that artists should include subjects seen within the modern city in their paintings, and went on to assert that the lower classes deserved to be represented in both portraiture and scenes of everyday life that were traditionally reserved for the aristocracy.[1] The manifesto which the press greeted with disdain, inspired a generation of art students in Paris. Whistler joined the discussions and debates about the nature and propriety of realist style and embraced the idea of representing the contemporary world about him.

In 1858, Whistler left Paris for London, moving to 62 Sloane Street to live with his stepsister Deborah Haden and her husband Dr. Francis Seymour Haden (ILLUS. P. 35). While there Whistler continued to engage the issue of realism within the context of his surroundings, and many friends, colleagues, and family members became the subjects of etchings that recorded his daily life, the places he frequented and the people with whom he spent time. Much of the work from this period, both prints and paintings, also reflects the relationship between Whistler and his brother-in-law. Haden gave the young artist access to his impressive etching collection, and the two worked closely together. Haden himself already was an accomplished etcher and inspired in Whistler a fascination with seventeenth-century Dutch and Flemish etchings, an affection that had already been nurtured by a visit to the great Manchester exhibition of 1857.

Around 1626, the remarkable Flemish painter and printmaker Sir Anthony van Dyck had begun to publish a series of engraved portraits of friends and fellow artists, under the title *Iconographia*, working in collaboration with publisher Martin van den Eden. Van Dyck sketched in the heads, barely indicated the bodies, and then turned the plates over to professional engravers for completion. Two centuries later, collectors vied for the proof impressions van Dyck had pulled prior to the publication of the plates.

As an admirer of van Dyck's work, Whistler completed several portraits that echoed van Dyck's approach and adopted a dark slashing drypoint stroke to create similar effects. One such intimate print represents sculptor Charles Drouet. Whistler and Drouet met as students in Paris during the 1850s and became lifelong friends, as Whistler fondly reflected four decades later.

> Oh Lord, he is a most extraordinary person! He is a sculptor & made a most extraordinary statue once of Ajax or something like that. He is a gourmet & can tell you where to go for good cooking in any town in France in which he has been at one time or another. He always had success, yet in our student days he would regard with horror the idea of taking a voiture when busses were to be had. Yet he is a most generous fellow, in a way, to his friends.[2]

Throughout his life Whistler maintained a close relationship with Drouet who, in 1896, sent a letter of condolence to Whistler after the death of the artist's beloved wife Beatrice. Drouet later assisted Joseph Pennell with detailed descriptions of Whistler's life as a student in Paris when Pennell was writing the biography of Whistler's life.

Reportedly Whistler needed just four hours in two sittings to complete Drouet's striking portrait.[3] He employed drypoint to produce the rich effects in the strong features and the detailed hair, capturing the strong personality of his sitter in this intimate portrayal. The informal delicate and harsh lines of Whistler's needle created the shadows and contours of Drouet's face that played off against the minimal contours of the body. The looser lines of the arms and torso, in three-quarter view, suggested the strength of the sculptor.

This print was received well by the contemporary British art world when it was singled out for praise when it was exhibited in 1874 at Whistler's first one-man show at Flemish Gallery, Pall Mall. Four years later during the legal proceedings against art critic John Ruskin, Whistler's solicitor, James Anderson Rose, presented this and eight other etched portraits as evidence of Whistler's skill as an artist.[4]

In the wake of his bankruptcy in 1879, Whistler cancelled the plate by crossing out the image with shallow drypoint lines. The plate was then sold to a commercial gallery, the Fine Art Society. The gallery had the cancellation lines polished away and hired another artist to reinforce the image. Impressions of the cancelled plate are abundant. These have faint parallel lines across the sitter's nose, a line across the collar, and near the right margin a short line above the date 1859. JWR

1. Champfleury, "Du Réalisme: Lettre á Madame Sand," *L'Artiste*, 16, no. 5 (1855).
2. Edward Kennedy, letter, June 7, 1897, Edward Guthrie Kennedy Papers, Manuscripts and Archives Division, The New York Public Library, Astor, Lenox and Tilden Foundations.
3. Pennell & Pennell, *Life of Whistler*, p. 49. Drouet assisted the Pennells in their biography of Whistler and may be the source of this.
4. James Anderson Rose, letter, November 25–26 1878, Pennell-Whistler Collection, Manuscript Division, Library of Congress, Washington, D.C.

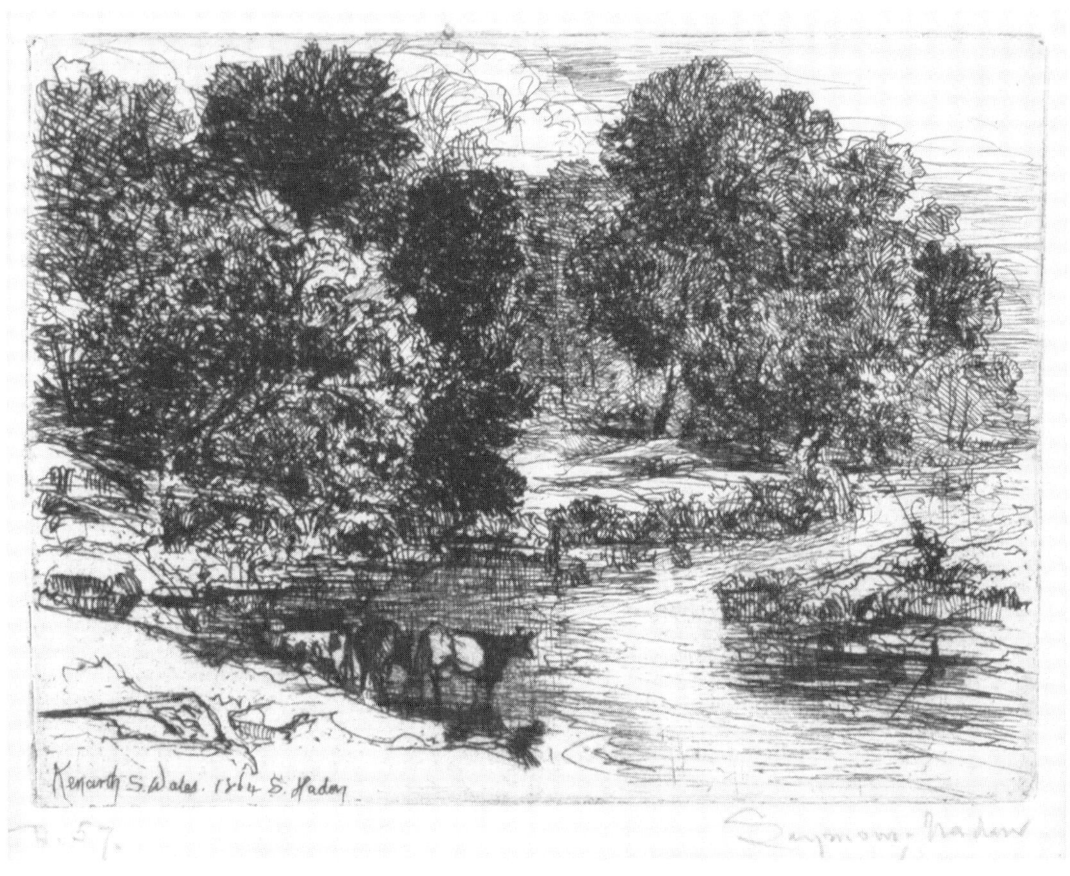

Kenarth, South Wales, 1864
Francis Seymour Haden (English, 1818–1910)
Etching on paper
Gift of Dr. and Mrs. Frederick Wolf
1970.21

Haden was an English surgeon and a printmaker who married Whistler's stepsister, Deborah, in 1847. He studied at the University College School and University College, London, and also at the Sorbonne in Paris. Admitted to London's College of Surgeons in 1842, he was self-taught as an etcher, and formed an impressive collection of historical etchings and engravings, which he made available to his brother-in-law for study.

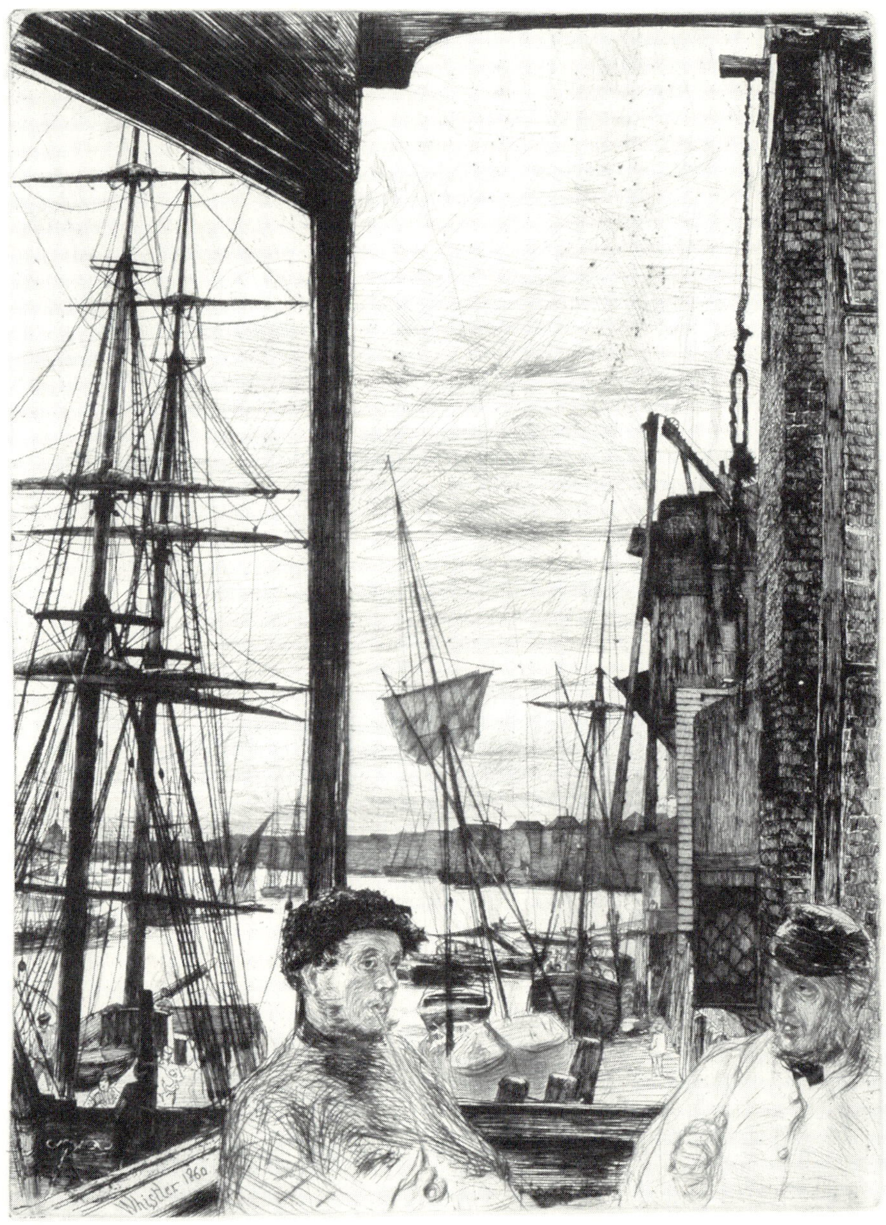

One of "Sixteen Etchings of Scenes of the Thames" (Thames Set)
Etching
Laid paper
Signed, recto, lower left in plate: "Whistler 1860"
Kennedy 66 iii/III; Mansfield 66
Checklist 21

Rotherhithe, 1860

CATALOGUE ENTRY 6

Thoroughly entrenched in the avant-garde realist aesthetic of Courbet, Whistler relocated from Paris to London in spring 1859. He soon discovered an appropriate subject in the life and activity of the working-class area along the lower reaches of the Thames. Working among the old wooden slips and docks, Whistler sought to capture the quotidian activity and appearance of the stevedores, sailors, and merchants of this district.

In *Rotherhithe* Whistler represented two men in conversation seated on the balcony of an inn overlooking the Thames. The northern banks of the river are visible in the distance beyond the elaborate rigging of the ships. The area beyond the water is Wapping, a district of London's East End where Whistler rendered other prints for the Thames set. In fact, Wapping was also the name the artist originally assigned to this etching when it was included in the set. The view in *Rotherhithe* was from the balcony of The Angel, an inn near Cherry Gardens on the south side of the river, almost directly opposite where Whistler executed two other plates: *Eagle Wharf* (CHECKLIST 11) and *Thames Police* (CHECKLIST 14, ILLUS. P. 39). The dome of St. Paul's cathedral is recognizable on the extreme left of the horizon, but its location is problematic, leading to difficulty in identifying the direction of Whistler's view. Most, though not all, of Whistler's topographical subjects are mirror images of the actual sites, due to the reversal of imagery during the printing process. Since this section of the city has been almost completely transformed, it is impossible to ascertain with certainty whether he drew the image in reverse or simply added the dome as a recognizable element of his composition. In either event, topography was clearly not Whistler's primary concern in this etching; the interaction of the two men, and the details of their surroundings assume the greater importance.

Rotherhithe is related to Whistler's *Wapping*, an oil painting of 1860–64 (National Gallery of Art, Washington, D.C.). The contrasts between how he treated these two similar subjects are instructive. The painting is horizontal and includes three figures that dominate the foreground of the composition. The etching is strongly vertical and includes only two figures in the lower quarter of the design. Whistler's preference for precision and realism is apparent in both, in the acute details of the balcony, the background, and the expressions of the models. In *Rotherhithe* the hatched lines of the buildings on the right brilliantly evoke the appearance of the aged brickwork, while balancing the rich black lines of the post and roof of the balcony. The detailed expressions and appearance of the two men are unusual in Whistler's prints, as well as the seventeen other figures beyond the balcony engaged in various riverside activities. During the early 1860s Whistler was profoundly influenced by Courbet's realism. However, the radical cropping of the foreground figures in the etching betrays one of the earliest indications of another potent influence on the artist: Japanese prints. As Whistler later said in closing his Ten O'clock lecture: "the story of the beautiful is already complete—hewn in the marbles of the Parthenon—and broidered, with the birds, upon the fan of Hokusai—at the foot of Fusiyama."[1]

Japanese woodblock prints exerted one of the most pervasive influences on Western art during the second half of the nineteenth century. Both the unusual subjects of the woodcuts and their unconventional style fired the creative imaginations of French, British, and American artists. With the coerced opening of Japan to Western trade in the 1850s, a market quickly developed for costumes, furnishings, and artwork from the mysterious and alluring Asian cultures. Japanese woodcuts began to appear in Paris in the 1860s in tea warehouses, curiosity shops, specialty shops such as La Porte Chinoise on Rue Vivienne, and shortly after in the grand department stores of the era. Although Japanese woodblock prints may first have appeared as wrapping for porcelain and other objets d'art, they were quickly recognized by artists for their unique depictions of Japanese life, and for their nonwestern stylistic elements. Many artists were influenced by the dramatic nonwestern perspective, strong colors, and arbitrary cropping found in the inexpensive woodblock prints. Whistler, Manet, Degas, Monet, and many other avant-garde artists working in France and England in the 1860s collected these prints, as did Mary Cassatt, Vincent and Theo Van Gogh, Gauguin, and Toulouse-Lautrec later. Asian art and aesthetics were enormously popular, exerting an enduring influence on European and American art throughout the final three decades of the nineteenth century. ED

1. As quoted in Thorp, ed., *Whistler on Art*, p. 95.98

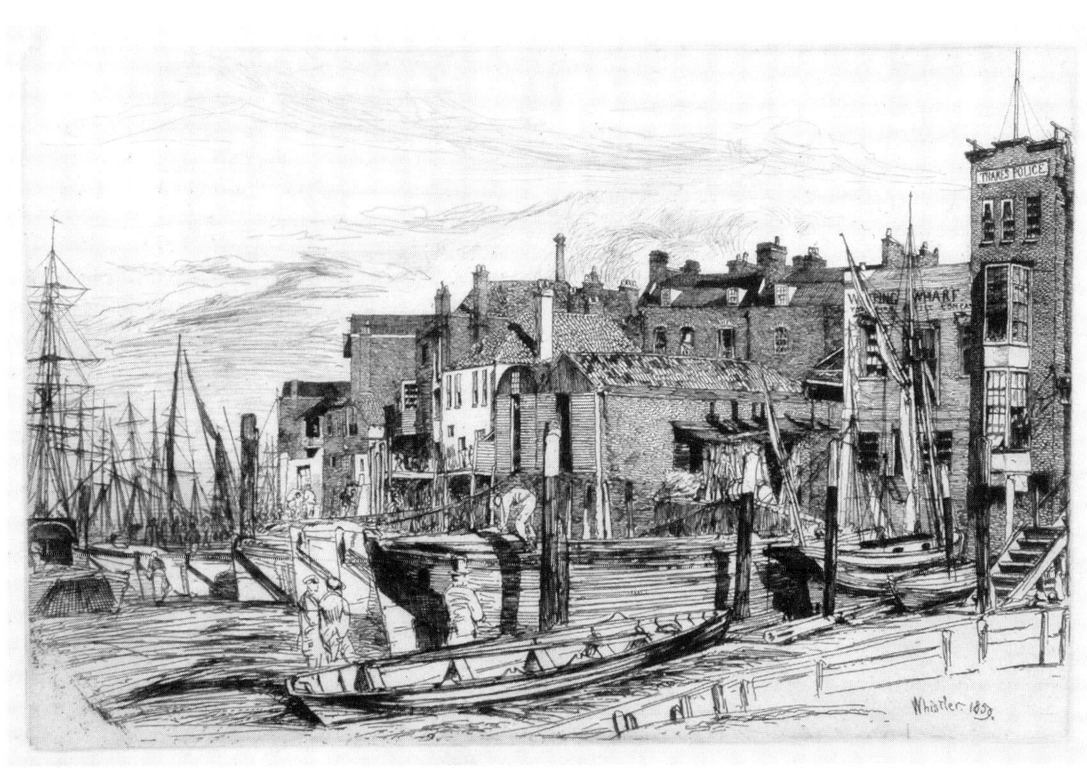

Thames Police (Third State), 1859
Etching on Japanese paper
Gift of Mr. and Mrs. Adolph Weil, Jr., in memory of Mr. and Mrs. Adolph Weil, Sr.
1984.17.7

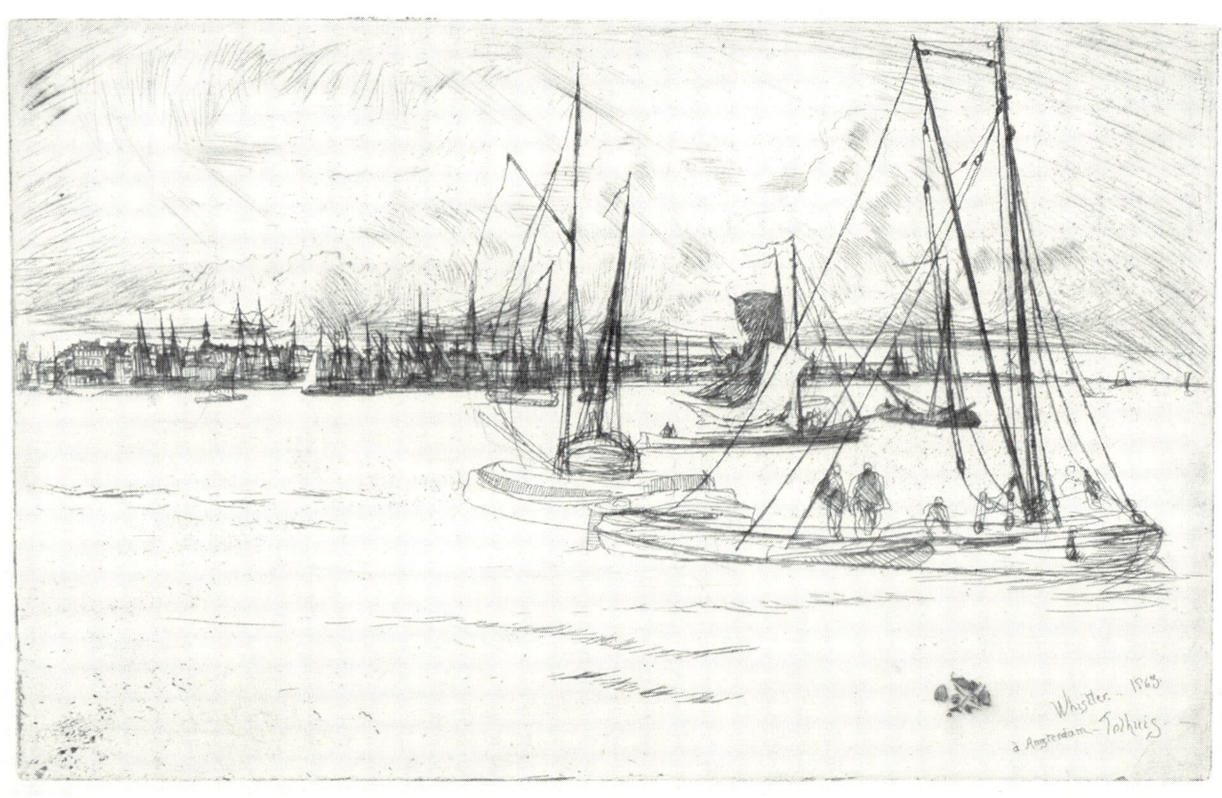

Etching and drypoint
Laid paper
Signed, recto, lower right in plate: "Whistler 1863" and artist's monogram (butterfly); lower right on sheet, in graphite: artist's monogram (butterfly) and "imp."
Kennedy 91 iv/IV; Mansfield 91
Checklist 28

Amsterdam, from the Tolhuis, 1863

CATALOGUE ENTRY 7

In *Amsterdam, from the Tolhuis*, Whistler looked across an expanse of water to the urban skyline, which Whistler represented as a narrow band of thickly condensed structures in the distance. The Tolhuis, a café, lay just beyond IJmuiden Canal (the IJ), the main shipping waterway linking Amsterdam to the North Sea. The café was not an easy destination; however, it provided marvelous views of the city, the vital shipping activity in the surrounding waters, and the structures on the islands of Kattenburg, Wittenburg, and Oostenburg.[1]

Whistler's choice of subject matter was in keeping with his approach at this time in other urban prints. As in the Thames Set he depicted "everyday" life in the commercial area, not the picturesque or tourist views. As usual, Whistler drew his image directly on the plate; the view in the etching thus represents a mirror image of the actual positions of the islands and their structures.

The year 1863 proved a significant one in Whistler's career. The artist, not yet thirty, had achieved both fame and notoriety. The year before, the Royal Academy in London had declined to exhibit his *The White Girl* (FIG. 1), an ambitious portrait of his mistress and model, Jo Hiffernan. In April 1863 the Salon jury in Paris rejected the same painting, along with a large number of other works by avant-garde painters and printmakers. When the artists petitioned the emperor, Napoleon III permitted them to show their work in the famous Salon des Réfusés, at which Whistler's *The White Girl* and Manet's *Luncheon in the Grass* were the two most celebrated paintings in the exhibition. In May 1863, Whistler traveled to The Hague to accept a gold medal for his prints in an exhibition that included twelve of his works and went on to Amsterdam in the company of Haden and fellow artist Alphonse Legros. Whistler and Haden, who had worked together for five years, found themselves increasingly at odds with each other, forcing Legros to act as an intermediary.[2] Perhaps these tensions kept the trip from being more productive—*Amsterdam, from the Tolhuis* is Whistler's only print from that trip. He and his brother-in-law never again etched together.

The image shows the unmistakable influence of Whistler's idol, Rembrandt, who had rendered distant views of Amsterdam in numerous prints and drawings, suggesting the thin foil of the city suspended between the surrounding waters and the moisture laden sky above. Yet, Whistler made dramatic changes to the copper plate over the next decades. Impressions of the first state had an extremely heavily worked sky, one of the most elaborate Whistler ever drew. Subsequently Whistler increasingly burnished and scraped down the heavy lines of the sky, replacing these with a delicate web of drypoint strokes to evoke lighter clouds. This and other changes reveal Whistler's evolving aesthetic, as he moved from dark and dramatic contour lines to a more suggestive use of line. The artist avoided the use of crosshatching for shadow throughout the print, and nothing in the composition is rendered in heavy detail. Whistler barely suggested the wraith-like pilots of the boats in the canal, and did little to differentiate between the buildings of the skyline and the masts of the moored ships. The movement of the water is rendered with very few strokes that indicate the currents and the waves.

About 1878 Whistler returned to the plate of *Amsterdam, from the Tolhuis*, which had never been published, to modify portions of the sky and add his butterfly signature to the copper. The MMFA impression is perhaps an even later print, as Whistler began to cut his etchings to the plate mark and leave a small tab for his pencil drawn butterfly only after his return from Venice in 1880. The Fine Art Society expressed some interest in publishing the print, as did the Gazette des Beaux-Arts in Paris, which wished to use the image in an article on Whistler; however, disagreements over the financial terms for reproducing the image prevented either from coming to fruition. Whistler's correspondence indicates that interest in *Amsterdam, from the Tolhuis* as an unpublished, fresh example of early work remained strong through the 1880s. EKJ

1. J. F. Heijbroek and Margaret MacDonald, *Whistler and Holland* (Zwolle: Uitgeverij Waanders; Amsterdam, Rijksmuseum, 1997), p. 50.
2. Lochnan, *Etchings of James McNeill Whistler*, p. 140.

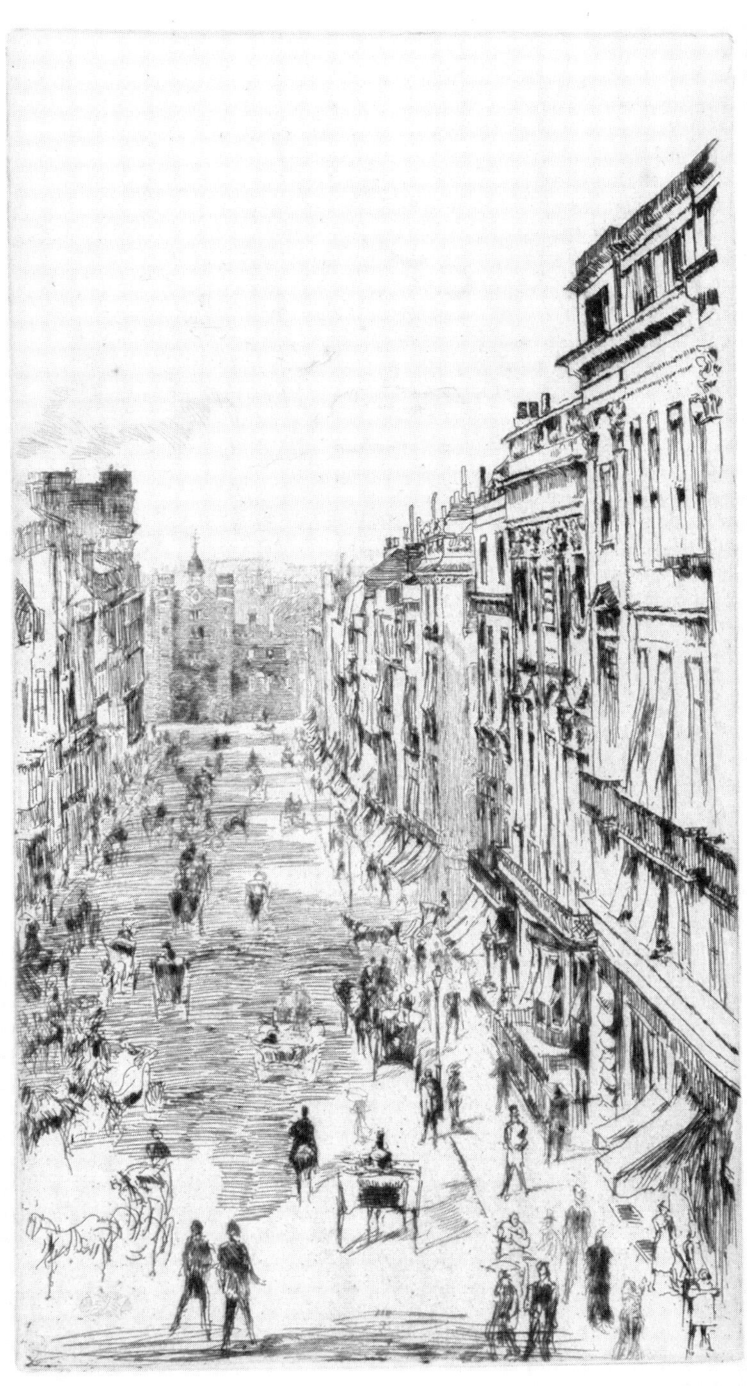

Etching and drypoint
Signed, recto, lower left in plate: artist's monogram (butterfly)
Kennedy 169 iv/IV; Mansfield 165
Checklist 31

St. James's Street, 1878

The broad thoroughfare of St. James's, located in central London, descends from a higher elevation on the north at Piccadilly to Pall Mall on the south. Originally a royal precinct, St. James's Palace was often the in-town residence of the monarchy during the eighteenth and nineteenth centuries. Henry VIII constructed the palace in the sixteenth century and, although no longer the monarch's residence, the Court retains its name as the Court of St. James. Just to the west of the boulevard, down short streets and alleys, lies Green Park, and just to the south, beyond the palace, are the Mall and St. James's Park.

Whistler represented *St. James's Street* looking south from the upper reaches of the fashionable neighborhood. As was his usual practice, he drew the design on a grounded plate directly from nature, so that the image was reversed in the printing process. On the right side of the etching he carefully rendered the elegant shops and clubs of St. James's Street, their awnings and their balustrades, leading down to the palace. Whistler composed *St. James's Street* using a single point perspective system, the orthogonals of the sidewalks and the rooflines of the buildings converge in the distance. He employed the sharp diagonal of the roofline on the right to create a sense of recession, and to lead the viewer's eye to the northwest corner of the palace. The white area of the plate just below the palace is Pall Mall then, as now, the home of some of the most notable clubs in London, places Whistler occasionally frequented. On the left side of the image the artist included the lower buildings of the west side of the street. Whistler depicted the image on a sunny afternoon, as indicated by the shadows cast by the buildings and the figures. For the most part he constructed the shadows with short parallel strokes, reserving his use of crosshatching for the rich black tones of the foreground carriages.

The artist populated this busy scene with more than seventy figures, including men in top hats, women with parasols, bobbies, and an array of coaches and carriages. The print captured contemporary life in a bustling area of London. In many ways, Whistler's etching was the graphic equivalent of the pioneering Parisian street scenes the impressionists had created earlier in the decade. Monet, Renoir, and Pissarro had all rendered the recently constructed elegant boulevards of Napoleon III's Second Empire. Monet's *Boulevard des Capucines* (1873) was one of the most notorious paintings in the first Impressionist exhibition of 1874. It represented the view looking down the wide boulevard from a balcony window at

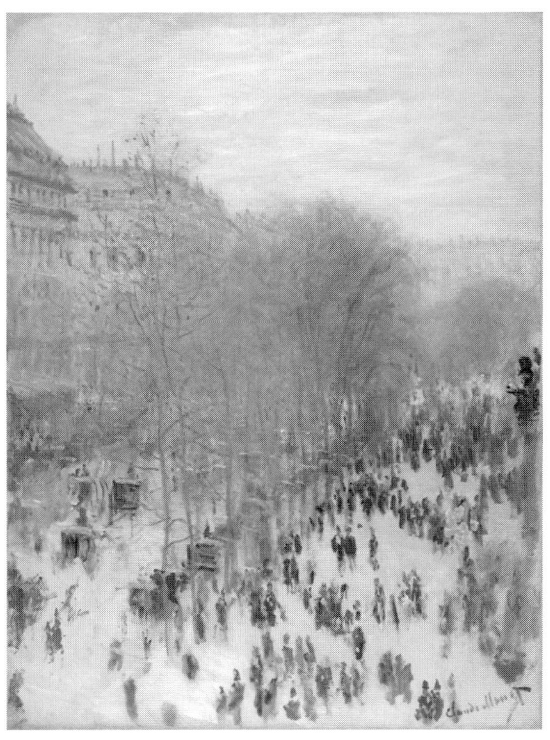

Boulevard des Capucines, 1873-1874
Claude Monet (1840-1926)
Oil on canvas, 31 5/8 x 23 3/4 in.
The Nelson-Atkins Museum of Art, Kansas City, Missouri
Acquired through the Kenneth A. and Helen F. Spencer Foundation Acquisition Fund, F72-35.
Photograph by Jamison Miller

photographer Nadar's studio (which also was the location of that first show). The conceptual parallels between Monet's painting and Whistler's etching are striking. Both utilize a high vantage point, and create a sense of depth by using the plunging diagonals of the roof lines and the streets to lead the eye into the distance. Both include numerous figures, the diverse inhabitants of the modern city economically suggested, and both indicate a specific time and weather. Whistler was well acquainted with Monet, Tissot, Fantin-Latour and other avant-garde French artists from his student days in Paris in the late 1850s, and regularly maintained contact with many of them throughout his life. He undoubtedly knew their paintings in the later 1870s, and *St. James's Street* reflects a similar aesthetic in their works. The organization of the etching also anticipates the structure of a number of Venetian plates, particularly the view in *The Rialto* (Kennedy 211) and *The Riva, No. 2* (CAT. ENTRY 17, P. 67).

Vanity Fair reproduced a lithograph of the etching in its June 1878 issue. In transferring the image to the stone, the composition was reversed so that it appeared in the periodical in the original orientation of the site, no doubt to the approbation of its readership. The MMFA's rich impression is signed on the lower left in the plate, as usual, with the artist's butterfly monogram. ED

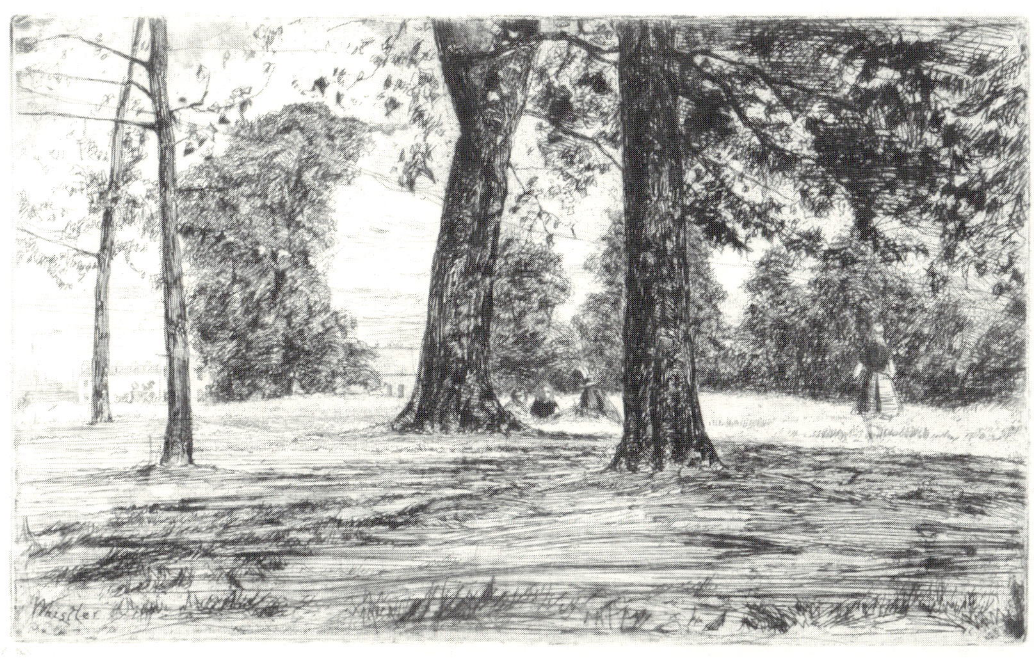

Greenwich Park (Second State), 1859
Etching on laid paper
Gift of Mr. and Mrs. Adolph Weil, Jr., in memory of Mr. and Mrs. Adolph Weil, Sr.
1992.2.22

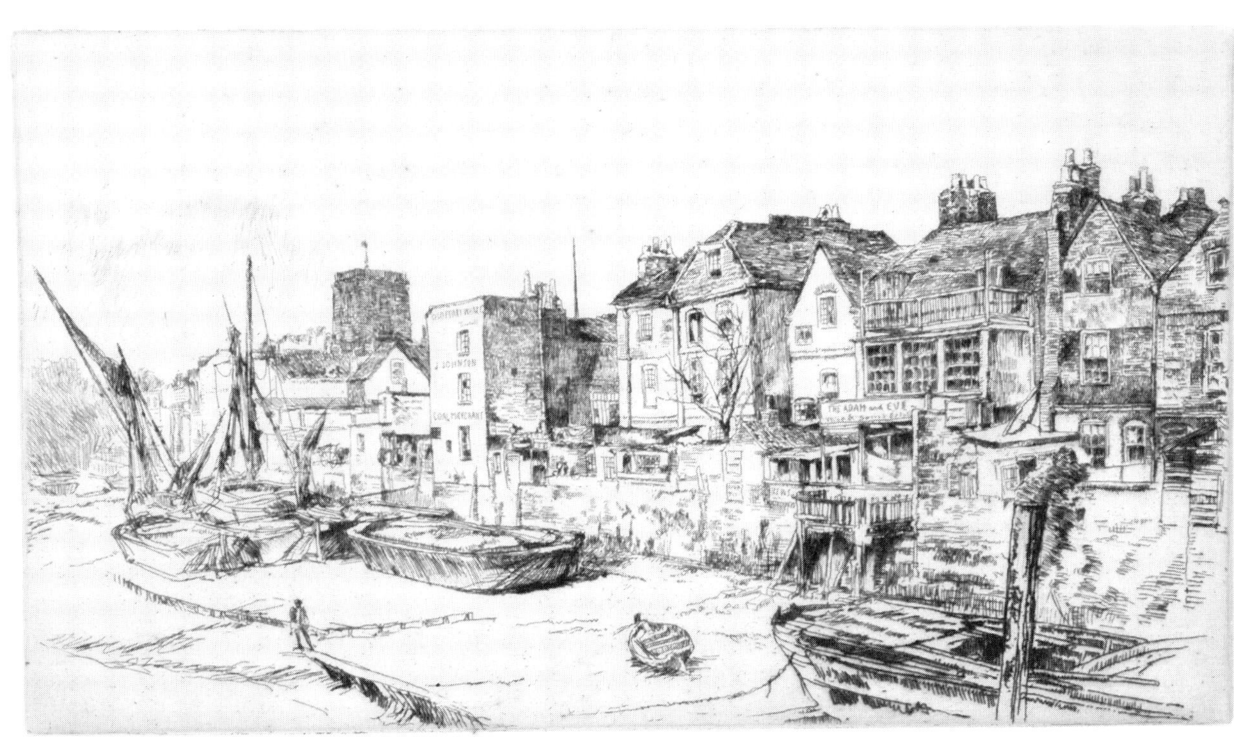

Etching
Laid paper
Signed, recto, upper left in plate: artist's monogram (butterfly)
Kennedy 175 ii/II; Mansfield 172
Checklist 32

The "Adam and Eve," Old Chelsea, 1879 CATALOGUE ENTRY 9

The late 1870s were a very difficult period in Whistler's career. His paintings did not sell, his relations with patrons had deteriorated, and art critic John Ruskin had lambasted Whistler's work in a published journal, prompting the artist to sue the critic for libel (see p. 18).

Whistler's financial condition, always fragile, worsened, and he went bankrupt in 1879. Hoping to recoup some of his financial losses, he decided to return to printmaking employing the style of the Thames Set of 1859–60, to date his most commercially successful endeavor. *The "Adam and Eve," Old Chelsea* was the first of the six etchings he completed and the only one not published by the Fine Art Society, his dealers.

To design the image, Whistler either etched from memory or used a photograph, as this part of the London waterfront had been torn down and rebuilt. Photographer James Hedderly had documented disappearing parts of London during the enormous urban revitalization programs of the 1860s and 1870s. He both lived and worked in Chelsea, and he was one of Whistler's creditors in the 1879. Although there are no records in the Whistler archives of the photographer's work, *The Adam and Eve, Chelsea*, a circa 1865 Hedderly photograph has much the same composition and details.[1]

Whistler's *The "Adam and Eve," Old Chelsea* is a densely etched image of the structures along the riverfront, probably viewed from a boat in the middle of the river. The title derives from the sign on a building on the right side of the composition. The artist emphasized the picturesque element of the old London waterfront, the buildings in different architectural styles, tightly amassed in an organic, unregulated manner. He underscored the old neighborhood's reliance on a river-based economy by giving prominence to the moored boats in the foreground. He included no figures in the etching, removing the sense of everyday life so central to the earlier Thames Set, and giving the image a degree of timelessness. Masses of hatching and crosshatching establish the dark tonal values in the shadows of the piers, the façades, and the roofs.

Whistler had specific rationale for his choices in style and subject matter. He was responding to imagery that was in high demand by the public, possibly for reasons of nostalgia for a part of the city that was gone forever. Yet his style had changed in the twenty years since the Thames Set. He no longer felt compelled to draw every detail but relied much more on suggestion, evoked by the use of shadows and small, but significant details. The sense of space and atmosphere result from Whistler's shift away from detailed realism to a more fluid and suggestive technique—*The "Adam and Eve," Old Chelsea* represents the transition from the linearity of Whistler's early etchings to the extremely economic, atmospheric handling of the Venetian works of 1879–80.

One interesting note on the provenance of this impression is that it comes to Montgomery from Kennedy Galleries in New York City, the commercial enterprise of art-dealer Edward G. Kennedy, who in 1910 issued the still standard catalogue raisonné of Whistler's etched work. EKJ

1. For more on the photographic source, see Nigel Thorp, "Studies in Black and White: Whistler's Photographs in Glasgow's University Library," in Ruth E. Fine, ed., *James McNeill Whistler: A Reevaluation, Studies in the History of Art*, vol. 17 (Washington D.C.: National Gallery of Art, 1987), pp. 96–98.

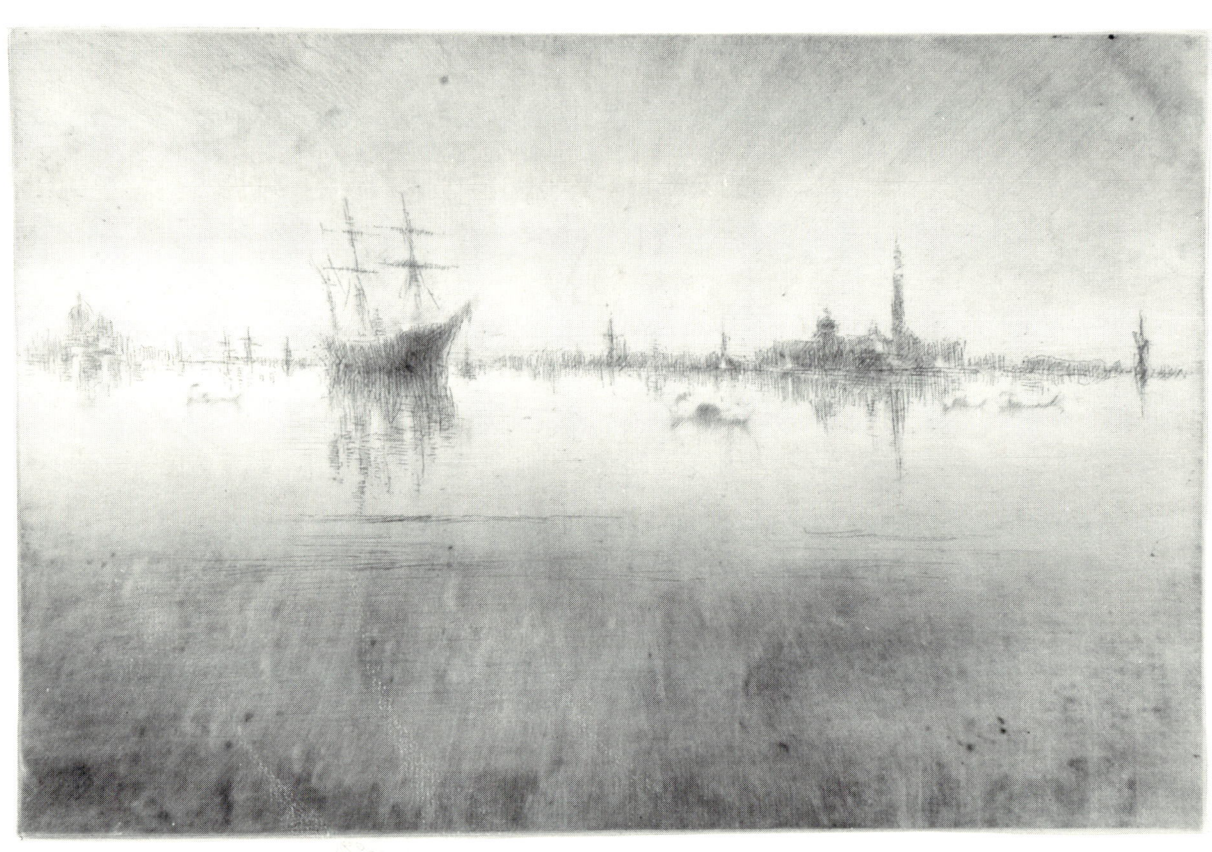

One of "Twelve Etchings" (First Venice Set)
Etching and drypoint
Laid paper
Signed, recto, lower left on tab, in graphite: artist's monogram (butterfly) and "imp."
Kennedy 184 iv/V; Mansfield 181
Checklist 34

Nocturne, 1879-80

CATALOGUE ENTRY 10

In the summer of 1879, as Whistler strove to recover from bankruptcy, he accepted an offer from the Fine Art Society in London to spend three months in Venice executing twelve etchings of the city that the society would market during the holiday season in England. Yet, soon after arriving in Venice he experienced difficulties developing an original approach to the city. As another expatriate American, writer Henry James opined just a few years later: "Venice has been painted and described many thousands of times, and of all the cities of the world is the easiest to visit without going there. Open the first book and you will find a rhapsody about it; step into the first picture-dealer's and you will find three or four high-coloured views' of it. There is notoriously nothing more to be said on the subject."[1] This familiarity did not stop either the talented author or the printmaker from attempting to say something new about the city, it simply delayed their estimation until they had something significant to produce.

Nocturne is an example of Whistler's panoramic treatments of Venice, a broad view across the basin of San Marco. To render this view, Whistler sketched on the plate looking southwest from the wide Riva degli Schiavoni at a position near Rio di San Martino, a canal not far from the Arsenale. Whistler lived close by in a boarding house, Casa Jankowitz on the riva in the sestiere (district of) Castello during the last five months he was in Venice. A high percentage of the prints originate in the vicinity of Whistler's rooms, although it is not possible to know with certainty if they were executed while he was living in the area.

In the distance, across the basin of San Marco, is Giudecca Canal. The domes and volutes of Baldassare Longhena's baroque votive church, Santa Maria della Salute, are described on the left side of the horizon; a three-masted schooner occupies a prominent place to the left of center. A ship's mast in the distance marks the exact center of the horizon line. On the right, balancing the schooner is the back of the church and campanile of San Giorgio Maggiore, the Palladian structure that dominates most views across the basin. Past several more isolated gondolas, another ship is represented on the far right, balancing the Salute on the left side of the print. As in all of Whistler's Venetian etchings, the view is a mirror image of the actual scene.

The artist limited the definition of the foreground and sky to a few spare horizontal lines, an occasional vertical added for variety of effect. Of special note is the sparse line work employed to define the ships, the building, and the horizon, conveying a sense of looking across the expanse of water into the distance. Whistler built upon this skeletal structure by clothing the scene in veils of ink during the printing process.

In each Venetian print Whistler varied the expressive possibilities of selected images by leaving a thin layer of ink on the surface of the copper during the printing process. Allowing ink to remain on the surface, outside of the lines incised into the copper, is referred to in printmaking as "selective wiping." An artist may subtly or dramatically change the image by use of selective wiping, creating what we would call today a monoprint. Although Rembrandt had also selectively wiped images in the 1600s, Comte Ludovic-Napoleon Lepic, who exhibited works in Paris in the 1870s in both the early impressionist exhibitions and the government sponsored official Salons, may have provided Whistler with more immediate inspiration. Although the process was already two hundred years old, it was Lepic who resuscitated the technique of monotype, the painting of ink on the surface of a blank plate to create one unique and unrepeatable printed impression. Lepic taught Degas and the impressionist circle monotype, and Whistler's use of selective inking, already seen to a limited degree in his early realist etchings, may have been reinforced by these colleagues.

In many of the Venetian etchings, Whistler carefully wiped each impression of the edition of one hundred to suggest varying effects of light (ILLUS. P. 51). In some heavily inked impressions Whistler sought to imply a time late in the evening; others he subtly wiped with insubstantial tone to evoke an earlier time in the afternoon. The medium-dark inking of the MMFA's impression of *Nocturne* suggests dusk, a favorite time of day for Whistler. The selectively inked prints Whistler executed in the Venetian sets mark Whistler's closest affinity to the aesthetics of Monet, Pissarro, and the landscape painters of the impressionist movement.

Whistler printed the impression in the MMFA in a dark brown ink on beige paper, a combination he regularly employed in the later states of the prints. Among the Venetian prints, *Nocturne* most closely resembles one of the few paintings Whistler brought back from his time in the city, *Nocturne in Blue and Silver: The Lagoon, Venice* (Museum of Fine Arts, Boston.) ED

1. Henry James, *Italian Hours* (London: William Heinemann, 1909), p. 1.

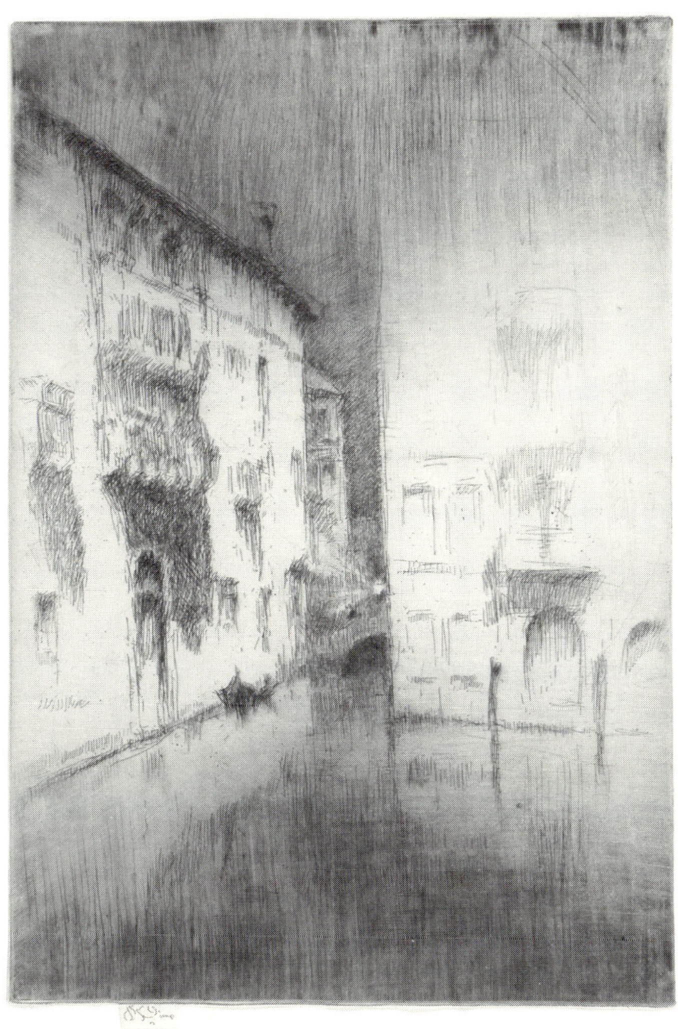

Nocturne: Palaces (Seventh State), 1879-80
Etching and drypoint on laid paper
Gift of Jean K. Weil in memory of Adolph "Bucks" Weil, Jr.
1999.7.143

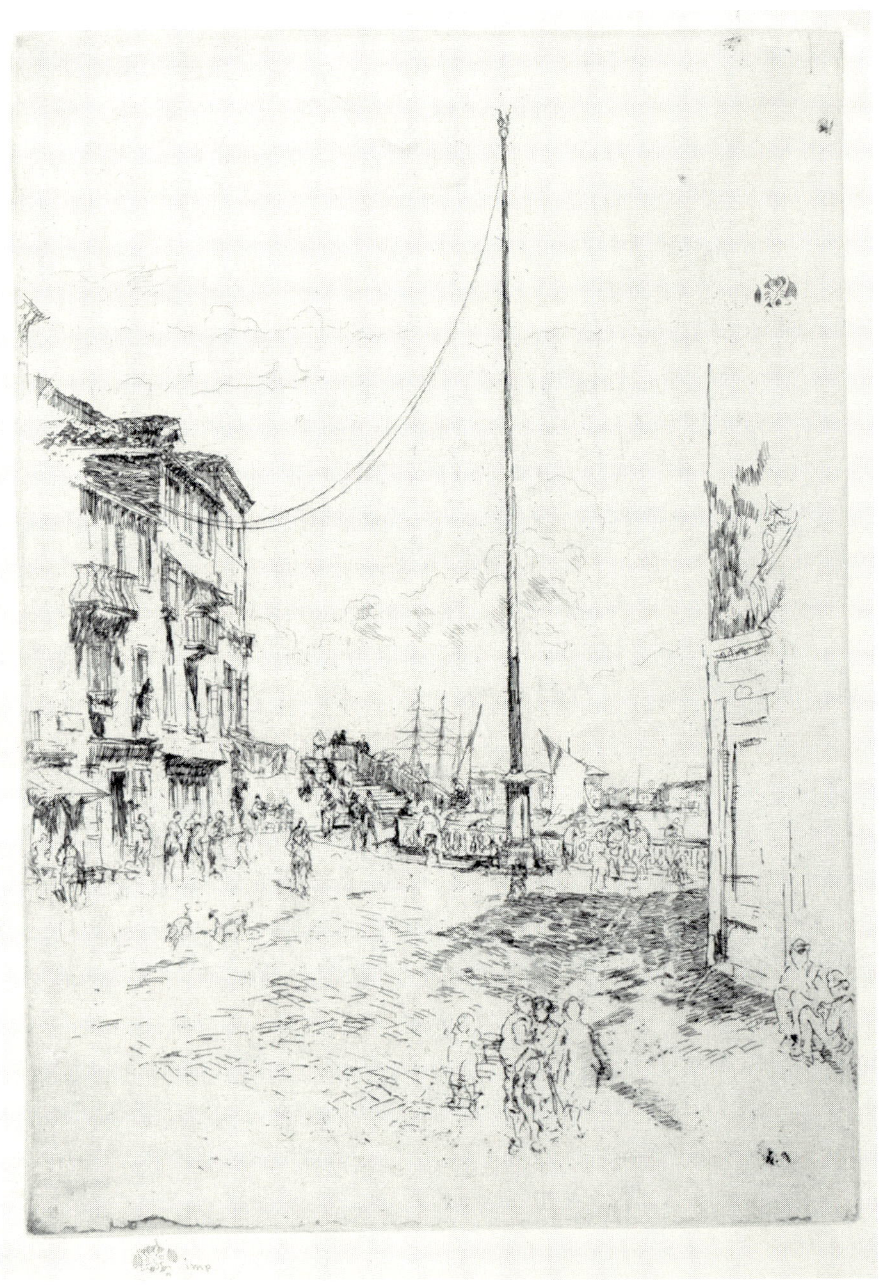

One of "Twelve Etchings" (First Venice Set)
Etching and drypoint
Laid paper
Signed, recto, upper right in plate: artist's monogram (butterfly);
lower left on sheet in graphite: artist's monogram (butterfly) and "imp."
Kennedy 185 iii/IV; Mansfield 182
Checklist 35

The Little Mast, 1880

CATALOGUE ENTRY 11

Whistler's Venetian subjects fall conveniently into a series of discrete categories: distant panorama of the city, economically defined and barely visible on the horizon as a foil between the sky and the lagoon; limited views of the corner of a square or courtyard; images of façades seen straight on across an indeterminate expanse of canal; an occasional oblique view down an obscure alley or canal, or perpendicular to an unremarkable bridge. *The Little Mast* is among those expanses of a court or street, a well-defined space that recedes into the distance.

The print depicts a humble space on the edge of a working class quarter of the sestiere Castello, at the western end of the wide Via Garibaldi, not far from where he lived. Insistently striving to capture a Venice of the Venetians, not simply the time worn and hoary images of the most familiar views of the city, he deliberately chose this nonceremonial spot rather than the familiar tourist areas around the monumental core of San Marco. Later, his compatriots Frank Duveneck and Otto Bacher also represented this section of one of the most impoverished neighborhoods of the city.

The view is a mirror image of the actual site. On the left are the heavily wrought buildings along the north side of the street, clearly recognizable today from the same spot. Whistler sat or stood on the south side of the street, an area in shadow at midday, while he sketched through the prepared plate; however, the inconsistent handling of the shadows suggests that Whistler sketched the plate at different times of the day. This is perhaps most apparent in the contrast between shadow of the solitary figure in the left middle ground, and the angle of the shadow of the mast that parallels the street.

Whistler carefully rendered the buildings on the left, differentiating the roofs and walls in a style that he had developed in the Thames Set, circa 1860. The artist employed no crosshatching anywhere in the image except on the base of the mast. In the left background, beyond the mast, is Ponte de la Veneta Marina—Whistler lived beyond this and a subsequent bridge on the quay. To the right of the mast, which is less diminutive than the title suggests, is the south side of the street, today the local post office. A network of parallel lines suggests the uneven ground of the unpaved street, but, as usual, the artist conveyed both the sky and the foreground with minimal drawing. Whistler's butterfly, drawn in reserve and surrounded by shadow, flutters about three-quarters of the way along the right edge.

Whistler printed almost all of the impressions of *The Little Mast* with no discernable surface tone. In the Venice sets, he generally cut each impression to the plate mark, leaving a small tab where he could draw his signature butterfly. That the impression of the print in the MMFA is not cut to the edge indicates it is outside of the editioned sets. This etching, in the penultimate of four recorded states, is one of several impressions that once belonged to the collection of the Royal Library in Windsor. ED

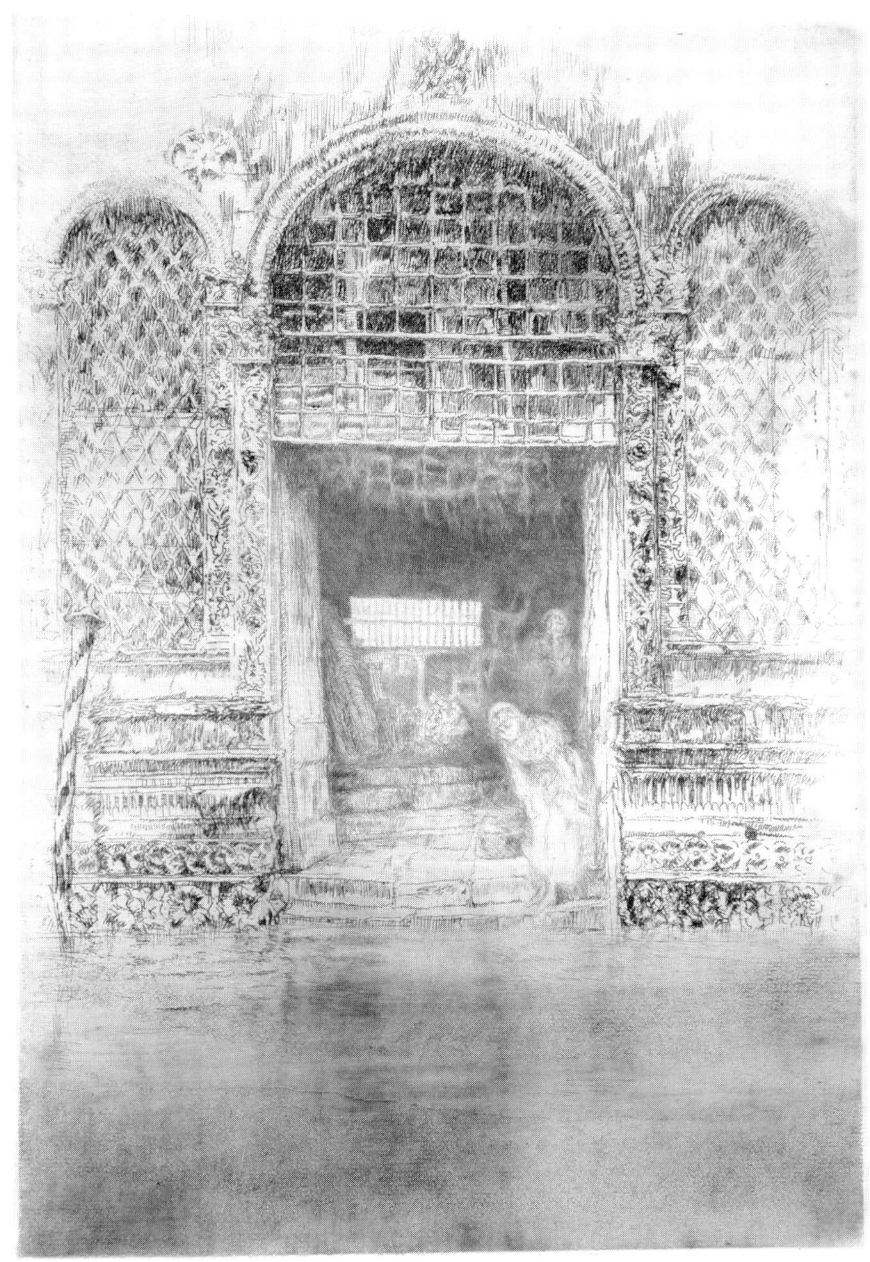

One of "Twelve Etchings" (First Venice Set)
Etching and drypoint
Laid paper
Signed, recto, upper left, in plate: artist's monogram (butterfly);
lower left on tab, in graphite: artist's monogram (butterfly) and "imp"
Kennedy 188 vi/VII; Mansfield 185
Checklist 36

The Doorway, 1879-80

CATALOGUE ENTRY 12

The Doorway is one of Whistler's most elegant Venetian etchings, successfully combining the artist's affection for detail and his innate sense of design to achieve a harmoniously balanced composition. The subject is the Renaissance Palazzo Gussoni on the upper reaches of Rio della Fava, a canal in the sestiere of San Marco. Whistler depicted the doorway of the palazzo from about ten yards away. The width of Rio della Fava at this point, just south of Ponte San Antonio, is about twelve yards. Although windows and an underpass open to the canal close to this spot, Whistler undoubtedly rendered this view from a boat, probably a gondola.

One of Whistler's favorite Venetian subjects was the close-up of a façade facing a canal, seen from a perpendicular angle across the water. *The Doorway* is a quintessential example of the artist's approach to this theme. Across a canal of seemingly indeterminate width, which yields no foreground indication of the artist's location, stands a precisely calculated section of a palace. The artist offered no visual clues to the size or structure of the remainder of the building. Instead, using a vertical format, Whistler focused attention upon the surface decoration of Istrian stone and Veronese marble, and the inherent geometry of the openings in the façade. He played these flat, two-dimensional effects against the sense of depth created by parallel planes beyond the portal, a space defined by light emanating from an inner courtyard and windows in the successive enclosures. The finely finished details of the stone carving, the grillwork, and the deep shadows of the interior contrast with the broad areas of uninterrupted copper in the upper and lower zones of the image.

On the MMFA's impression of *The Doorway*, Whistler left a rich layer of ink in the foreground to suggest turbid water in the canal. He also left a thin veil of ink on parts of the façade, yielding less contrast to the dark shadows of the doorway than in other impressions of this print. Whistler included his trademark butterfly etched on the wall above the window on the left, cleverly introducing it as if it were carved into the marble façade.

Whistler believed that he had developed a new approach to composition while drawing his Venetian scenes, which Australian Mortimer Menpes later recollected:

> [Whistler] described how in Venice once he was drawing a bridge, and suddenly, as though in a revelation, the secret of drawing came to him. He felt that he wanted to keep it to himself, lest someone should use it,—it was so sure, so marvelous. This is roughly how he described it: "I began first of all the chief point of interest,—the little palaces and the shipping beneath the bridge. If so, I would begin drawing that distance in elaborately, and then would expand from it until I came to the bridge, which I would draw in one broad sweep. If by chance I did not see the whole of the bridge, I would not put it in. In this way the picture must necessarily be a perfect thing from start to finish. Even if one were to be arrested in the middle of it, it would still be a fine and complete picture."[1]

One of the singular characteristics of Whistler's Venetian work is the elaboration of the central motif, the focal point of a design that expanded out from the middle but not to the edges of the plate. His predilection for detailing only the important elements of the design, while leaving the marginal and other areas incomplete, was part of the avant-garde nature of his art, inspired in large part by Japanese print aesthetics that included the employment of radical cropping and a reduction to the most essential parts of a motif for design purposes.

Otto Bacher, one of Frank Duveneck's students working in Venice with Whistler during the summer of 1880, wrote of this print, "The exquisite beauty in this proof consists in its wonderfully accurate detail of the carving and fretwork, even to the spider-webs. On one occasion, Whistler asked me if I knew what was hanging from the ceiling. I told him that they looked like rush-bottomed chairs, which was entirely correct. He often asked questions of this kind in order to make sure that he was describing rightly to other eyes."[2] ED

1. Menpes, *Whistler as I Knew Him*, pp. 22–23.
2. Bacher, *With Whistler in Venice*, pp. 193–94.

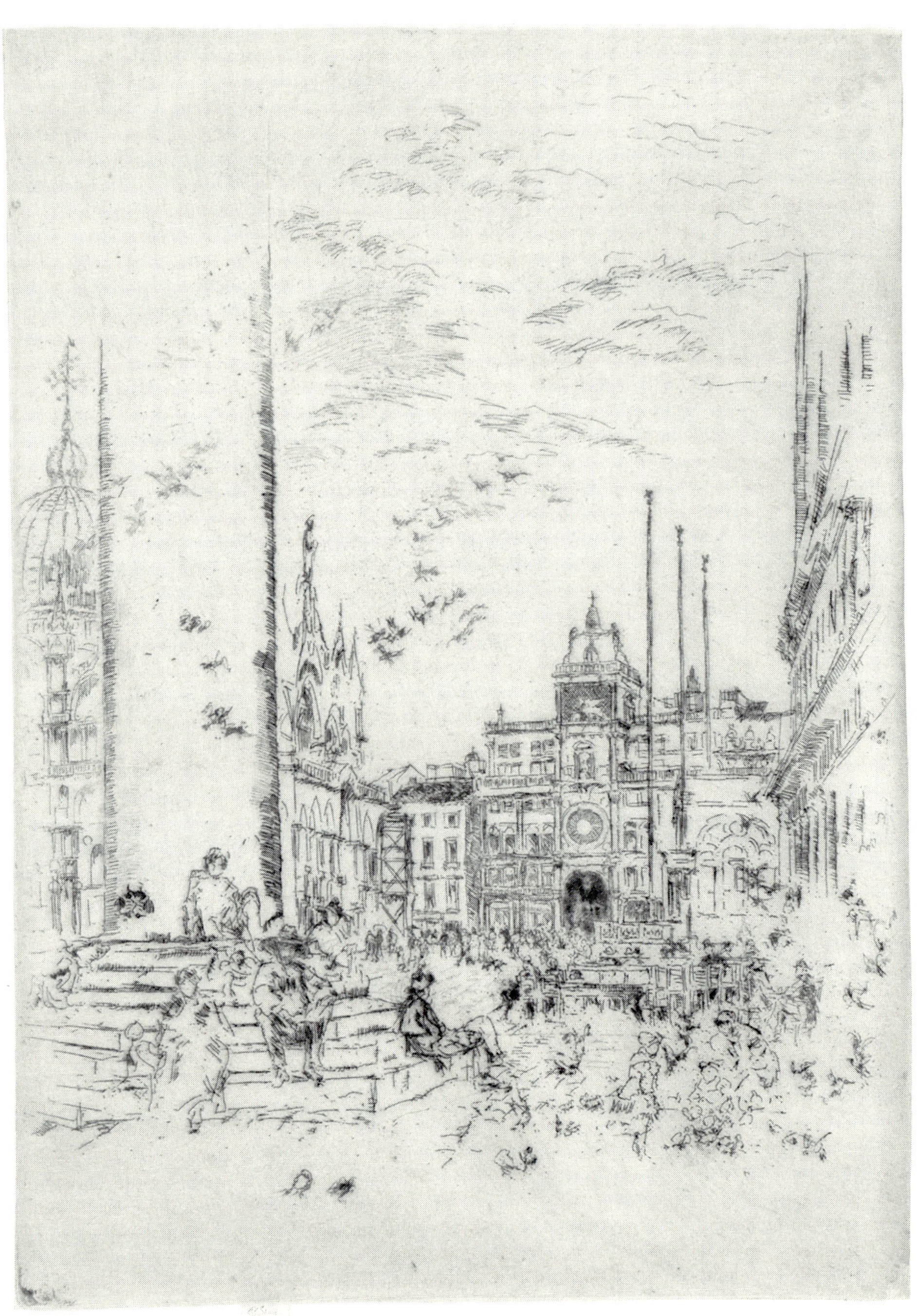

One of "Twelve Etchings" (First Venice Set)
Etching
Japanese paper
Signed, recto, lower left in plate: artist's monogram (butterfly); lower left on tab, in graphite: artist's monogram (butterfly) and "imp."
Kennedy 189 iii/V; Mansfield 186
Checklist 37

The Piazzetta, 1879-80

CATALOGUE ENTRY 13

The Piazzetta is one of Whistler's rare images of the ceremonial, political, and religious center of Venetian life: Piazza San Marco and its adjacent piazzetta. The artist depicted the view from the southwest corner of the piazzetta looking northeast, from the wide quay known as the Molo, beyond the present day Grand Café Chioggia. The domes and pinnacles of the façade of Basilica of San Marco are on the left, partially obscured by one of the two great columns that greet the visitor entering from the basin of San Marco. The two columns support statues of the patron saints of the Republic, the first patron saint of the city Saint Theodore, and the later and more prestigious protector of the city, Saint Mark the Evangelist. The view is past the more westerly of the two columns, although Whistler cropped the column before it reaches its apex. The Renaissance clock tower of San Marco, designed by Mauro Codussi, stands in the center of the composition. In front of the clock tower are the three great flag posts of the Republic and the loggetta, the small guardhouse for the campanile designed by Jacopo Sansovino. Marciana Library, also by Sansovino, closes the composition on the right. Whistler omitted the campanile almost entirely, as he did the upper part of the library, to focus attention on the lower part of the image. The lack of shadows suggests midday.

In this case, as in all of the Venice etchings, he drew his image directly on the prepared surface of his copper plate, knowing that the printing process would produce a mirror image of his drawing. In this way, he sought to avoid the attraction of this print as an illustration of the site, confounding those nineteenth-century collectors who wanted only a recognizable view. He rejected the notion of creating a series of recognizable views more valued for their subjects than for their artistic accomplishment. His goal was to find a Venice in Venice that was unknown to visitors, one that embodied the experience of the city from the viewpoint of the residents. When he did tackle a recognizable view, as here, he employed an unconventional angle, an unusual vantage point, and focused attention on aspects of everyday life, from the indolent figures on the steps at the base of the column to the children playing in the right foreground to the habitués of the cafe in front of the library.

The MMFA's impression of *The Piazzetta* is printed in dark brown ink on a cream color paper. The plate was cleanly wiped during inking, leaving no surface tone, as is common in the printing of this image. Despite Whistler's reputation for economy of detail, and his preference to evoke rather than define, *The Piazzetta* offers a number of intriguing details, such as the scaffolding erected to allow cleaning and restoring of the mosaics at Basilica of San Marco. Whistler also

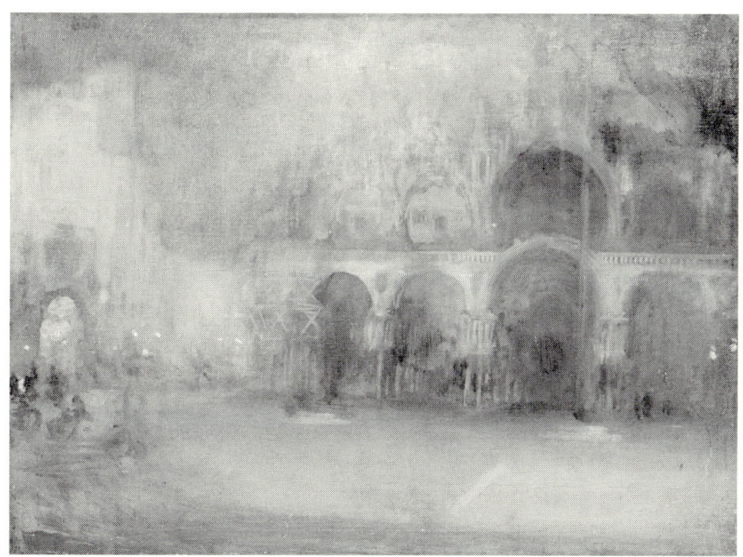

Nocturne: Blue and Gold—St. Mark's, Venice, 1879-80
Oil on Canvas, 17 1/2 x 23 1/2 in.
National Museum and Gallery of Wales, Cardiff

included it in one of the two remaining paintings of the Venetian period, *Nocturne: Blue and Gold—St. Mark's, Venice*. As a realist artist in his twenties, Whistler had been among the first artists to use scaffolding as a pictorial element in their work. In this, he may have been influenced by Charles Meryon, the great Parisian printmaker who captured the old city as it underwent modernization and renovation (ILLUS. P. 59). Whistler's paintings and prints that illustrate temporary supports and scaffolding may be responsible for a generation of later artists repeatedly employing the theme including Mortimer Menpes, Joseph Pennell, and, some years later, printmaker Muirhead Bone. Meryon's images are often ominous, and Whistler's flurry of pigeons to the right of the column is reminiscent of the French printmaker's darker scenes without reviving the same tone.

The way in which Whistler truncated the foreground column may signify the influence of another artist. When Whistler first arrived in Venice, he lived near the Franciscan church of the Frari, which houses two of Titian's Renaissance masterpieces, *Assumption of the Virgin* over the high altar, and the votive *Pesaro Altarpiece*. In the latter, Titian created a grand architectural setting with an immense column that soars into space above. Pictorially Whistler's truncated column balanced the library on the right side of the scene, but it may also have been inspired by Titian's use of architecture, for as the Pennells reported in their biography, Whistler thought Veronese and Titian "great swells."[1] ED

1. Pennell & Pennell, *Life of Whistler*, p. 263.

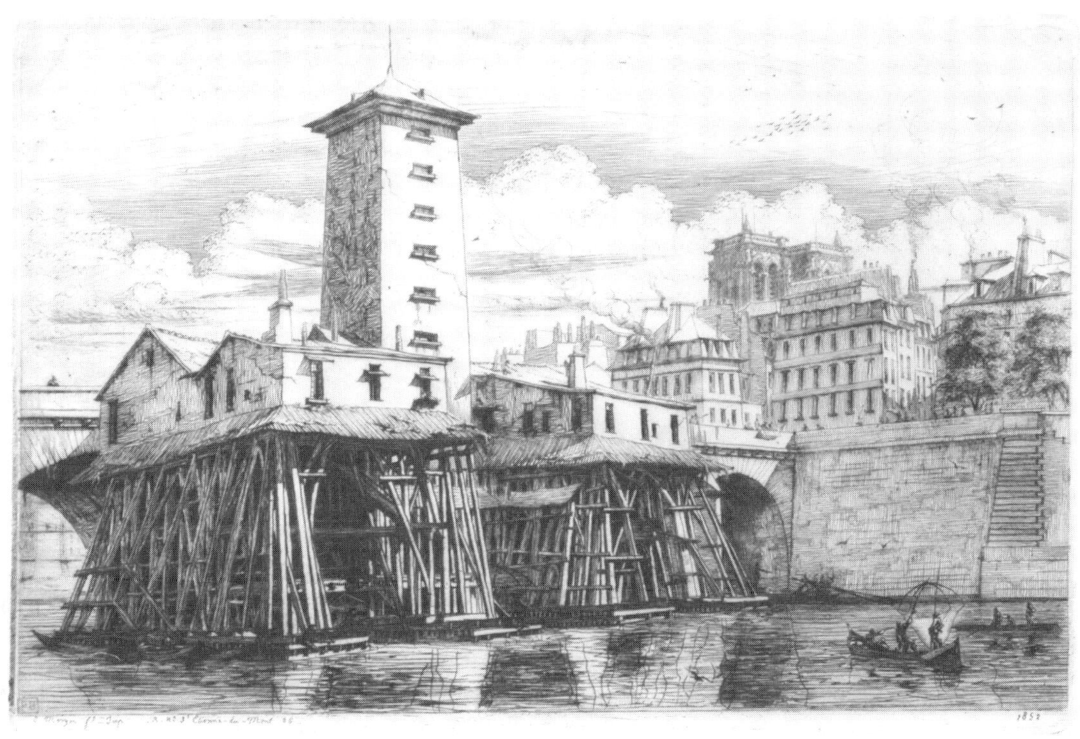

La Pompe Notre-Dame, 1852
Charles Meryon (French, 1821-68)
Etching and drypoint on paper
Gift of Mr. and Mrs. Adolph Weil, Jr., in memory of Mr. and Mrs. Adolph Weil, Sr.
1999.7.143

The etching revival in Europe was partially inspired by the work of an eccentric artist and printmaker, Charles Meryon. The illegitimate son of an English doctor and a dancer in the Paris Opera, Meryon was a graduate of the French navel academy who discovered the etching technique in 1848. He created a body of work illustrating Paris in the 1850s and early 1860s as it transitioned to a modern city. His style was precise and dynamic, with a fresh, linear quality that captured Whistler's attention. One of his favorite landmarks was the church of Notre Dame, shown here in the background, with an adjacent river pumping station.

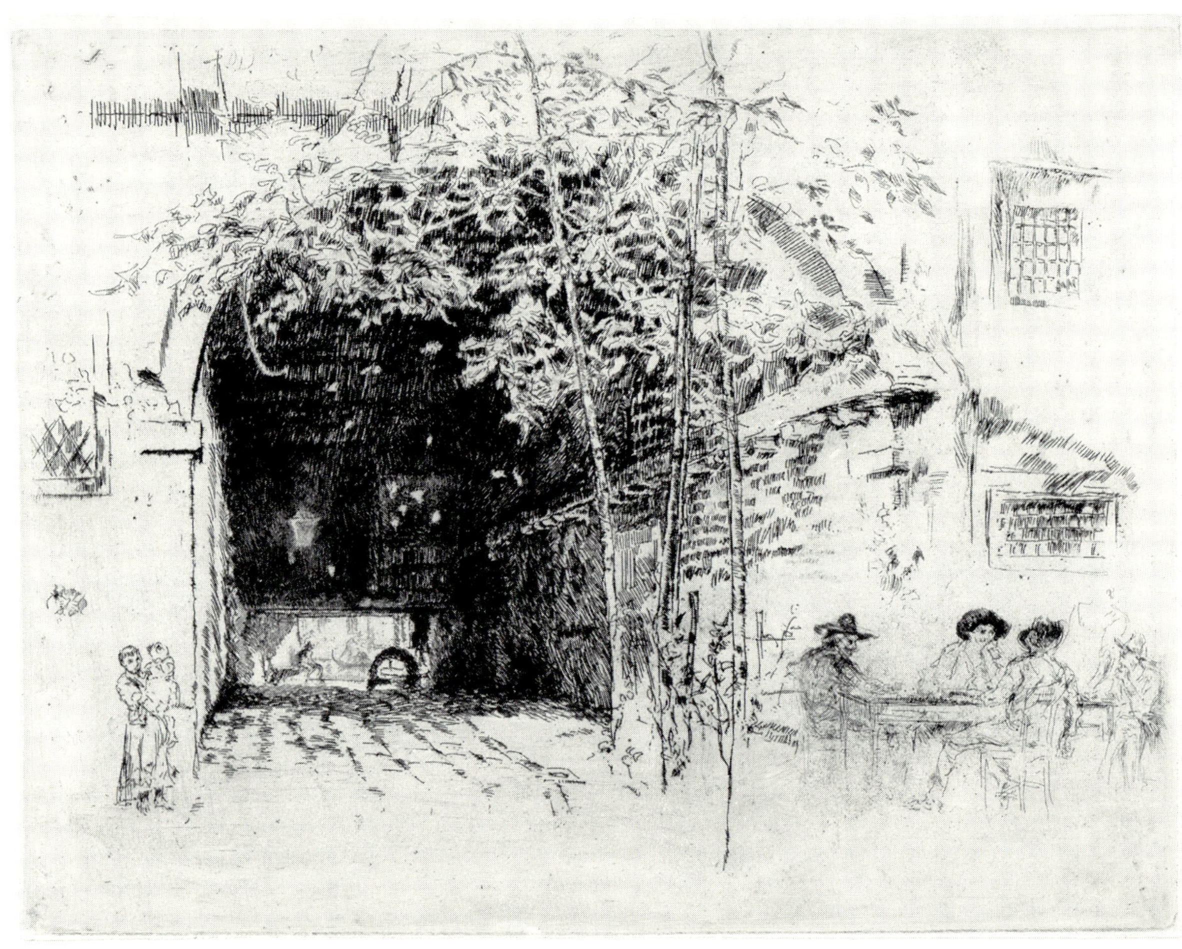

One of "Twelve Etchings" (First Venice Set)
Etching and drypoint
Laid paper
Signed, recto, left center on plate: artist's monogram (butterfly) and "imp."
Kennedy 191 iii/IV; Mansfield 188
Checklist 38

The Traghetto, No. 2, 1879-80

CATALOGUE ENTRY 14

Whistler often searched out isolated courts and alleyways to sketch. He drew the image for *The Traghetto, No. 2*, in a tranquil court off the heavily trafficked route from Rialto Bridge to Strada Nova, at the time called Via Vittorio Emmanuelle. The courtyard is located in the southeastern corner of the sestiere of Cannareggio not far from its border with the sestiere of San Marco, near Church of Santissimi Apostoli. He sat in Corte del Leonbianco, behind palazzo Ca' da Mosto, just off of the Grand Canal. The traghetto of the title is a gondola ferry that crossed the Grand Canal, although by Whistler's time this was no longer the site of the service.

The Traghetto, No. 2 presents an interesting variation on Whistler's theme of enclosed courts and closely cropped images in the corners of public spaces. The artist represented a large archway daringly left of center in what appears a broad open space with a few leafy trees. The dark interior of a passageway is balanced by several windows on the façade and a group of men seated around a table to the right. The illumination from the far end of the archway silhouettes a gondolier rowing on the Grand Canal, a barely described seated figure at the end of the tunnel, a hanging lamp, and a felze, the traditional top to a gondola that provided shelter for passengers. Today, the arch is closed off by a metal grate, and the passageway is littered with junk, but the boxlike storage area in the upper left remains. Barely visible across the canal is the Fabriche Nove of the Rialto markets. Whistler sat on the opposite quay to draw the front of Ca' da Mosto, along with this etching one of his very few scenes that include the Grand Canal.

The artist depicted the scene in the late morning or early afternoon when the sun was high and penetrated into the passageway. Whistler located himself and the viewer facing west, in the middle of what seems a broad street or the end of a square, near a sotoportego that led to a canal. He offered no visual clues to the near foreground, paralleling his treatment of the water in the scenes of façades fronting on canals. In fact, Whistler radically reconfigured the actual space. The location is a small, almost claustrophobic courtyard.[2] The artist placed his back against the far wall of the square; just out of view to the left is an exterior staircase leading to the next level, and just out of view to the right is the end wall. The etching offers no idea of the extent of the building, neither its height nor its stature. As usual, Whistler drew directly on the plate, so that the etching is a mirror image of the actual scene.

A dark underpass leading to a passage of bright light in the distance had been a favored motif of the artist since his early etched sets. *The Kitchen* (CAT. ENTRY 2, P. 27) from the French Set, and *The Lime-Burner* (CHECKLIST 16, ILLUS. P. 116) from the Thames Set contain similar devices, as does *The Doorway* (CAT. ENTRY 12, P. 55) in the Venice etchings.

Otto Bacher, a follower and friend of Whistler living in Venice in 1880, later explained the "*No. 2*" that makes this an unusual title. When Whistler initially etched the plate he printed a few delicate impressions. He then reworked the plate, but the printing of the altered copper left the artist dissatisfied. Instead of continuing to work on the plate, he transferred the image by taking an impression inked with white paint, and applied that impression to the dark ground of another plate so that he could recreate the original image. This allowed him to scrupulously redraw the subject, using the white proof as his guide. Whistler then added drypoint to some areas to reinforce the etched lines.[2]
ED

1. Grieve, *Whistler's Venice*, p. 84. I am indebted to Alastair Grieve's identification for the sites of Whistler's etching.

2. Bacher, *With Whistler in Venice*, pp. 169–80.

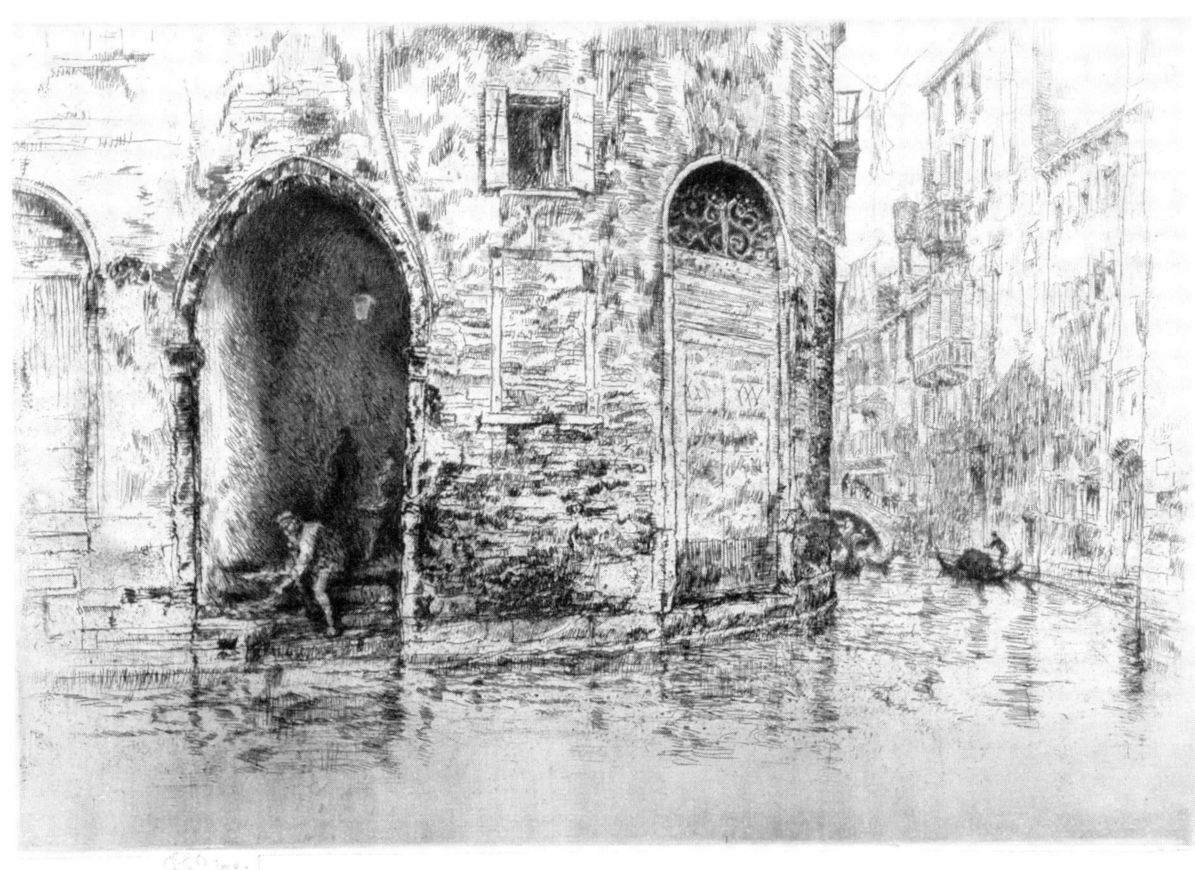

One of "Twelve Etchings" (First Venice Set)
Etching and drypoint
Laid paper
Signed, recto, upper left in plate: artist's monogram (butterfly);
lower left on tab, in graphite: artist's monogram (butterfly) and "imp."
Kennedy 193 iv/VI; Mansfield 190
Checklist 40

Two Doorways, 1879-80

Whistler rendered many of his Venetian views from a gondola, floating only a few feet above water level, a characteristic viewpoint for nineteenth-century visitors. For *Two Doorways* the gondola floated at the intersection of the three districts that comprise the northern and eastern part of the city, Cannareggio, San Marco, and Castello. Looking southwest, he depicted the junction of Rio della Fava and Rio dei Fondaco dei Tedeschi; Rio di San Lio stretched behind the artist to the north. As usual, Whistler did not bother to reverse the image on the plate, so the view in the etching mirrors the actual site.

The façades of buildings along Rio della Fava extend into the distance on the right, with one end of Ponte San Antonio visible. (Whistler drew the etching of *The Doorway* [CAT. ENTRY 12, P. 55] beyond the bridge on the eastern side of the canal.) Above that bridge, the narrow slice of sky silhouettes laundry hanging over the canal. The center of the plate is dominated by the two large doorways of the title, the left one being the end of Ramo de l'Orso, an underpass leading to Corte de l'Orso. This area of San Marco is a dense warren of narrow streets many of which unexpectedly culminate at water's edge. The two doorways are represented on the rounded rear façade of a building that follows the irregular shape of the canals. Unlike the perpendicular view that he generally favored for canal side images, on this one Whistler allowed the dominant central façade to curve out of the viewer's sight at an unusual angle.

Two Doorways is one of the most heavily wrought of all of Whistler's Venetian etchings. Whistler employed his usual parallel line work to convey the sense of afternoon sunlight and shadows playing across the façades to the right; however, the line work became heavier as he described the irregular surface of the dilapidated walls of the curved façade. He delighted in the distinctions between the aging wood of the door, the iron scrollwork above the door and the brickwork and mortar of the ancient dilapidated façade. On the heavily drawn canal side opening at the end of Ramo de l'Orso, he used cross-hatching and multiple hatched networks, some applied with drypoint. Whistler wanted to suggest something slightly sinister in the deep shadows inhabiting the passageway. Attuned to nuances that could change the artistic impact, he evolved the image through a number of different stages in its development before he pronounced himself satisfied. A gondola with two men appeared then disappeared in front of the doorway. Two female figures materialized in the shadows above the steps only to then vanish in the intermediate stages. Later, an old man appeared on the steps bending toward the left, and a girl holding a basket reappeared in the shadows of the doorway. In the final state of the print, a second figure joins the young woman in the doorway. The MMFA's impression of *Two Doorways* is from a stage prior to the finished print, as indistinct figures appear in the doorway. Printed in brown ink on cream paper, a slight veil of ink gave tone to the water.

Otto Bacher made an etching in a gondola close by, around the corner on Rio del Piombo, looking to the east at Ponte del Pistor. When reminiscing about his time in Venice with the artist, Bacher recalled this canal was "A favorite spot of Whistler's."[1] ED

1. Bacher, *With Whistler in Venice*, p. 95.

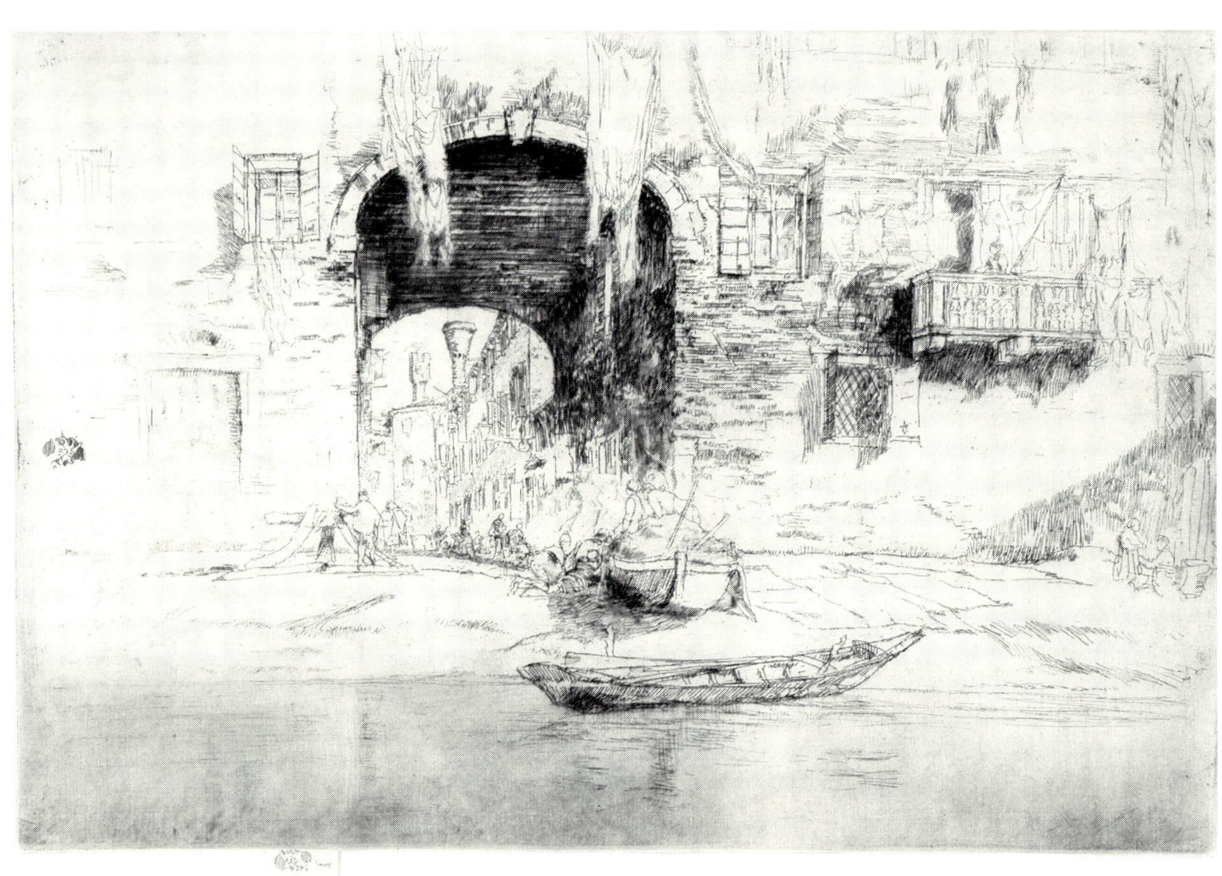

One of "Twenty-Six Etchings" (Second Venice Set)
Etching and drypoint
Laid paper
Signed, recto, center left in plate: artist's monogram (butterfly);
lower left on tab, in graphite: artist's monogram (butterfly) and "imp."
Kennedy 197 ii/IX; Mansfield 194; proof state, not from published set
Checklist 43

San Biagio, 1879-80

CATALOGUE ENTRY 16

San Biagio is set in the sestiere Castello on the long quay that stretched southeast from Molo in front of Piazza San Marco and terminated just beyond Strada Nuova dei Giardini (present day Via Garibaldi), just east of where Whistler lived in the last five months of his stay in Venice. Beyond the quay stood a collection of ramshackle buildings and squeros (boatyards) fronted by a short slope of land that allowed boats to be pulled ashore for work, and one prominent block of buildings, containing the Calle and Corte de la Colonna, that provided low-income housing.

The southwest façade of the complex is penetrated by two imposing arches that frame the underpasses providing access to the interior spaces. The Church of San Biagio stands one hundred and fifty yards northwest, adjacent to Casa Jankowitz where Whistler lived. Why Whistler gave the plate this title remains unclear; however, he may have simply conflated the two places by 1886 when he decided to include the etching in the Second Venice Set.

Whistler depicted the western of the two arches from a low vantage point, which intimates he worked from a boat or perhaps sat on a sandbar at low tide. In the foreground is a two-man sandolo, a flat-bottom boat commonly used in the lagoon both in Whistler's time and today. Behind the sandolo is a larger boat with two boys on top and several more in the shade cast by the afternoon sun. The boys on the ground play some kind of game, perhaps cards or gambling, and have attracted the attention of the boys above. Other diminutive figures along the water and through the arch continue their everyday activities: working, playing, making lace. Looming over the human activity is the great dark entrance to the interior streets and courts of the block. Whistler cropped the sides and top of the building, as was his custom, isolating the geometry of the façade from the limits of the structure.

With great economy Whistler suggested the brick and mortar work of the wall, the windows, the balcony, the grillwork in the windows, and the gowns hanging down outside the arch. The heavy crosshatching that conveys deep afternoon shadow offers a brilliant foil for the sunlight playing across the adjacent façades.

The MMFA's impression, a rare early proof of the print, may be unique. Early in the twentieth century, distinguished Whistler collector Henry Harper Benedict owned it, and it may be the actual impression reproduced in Edward Kennedy's 1910 catalogue raisonné.[1]

In 1880 American artist Frank Duveneck, who spent time with Whistler in Venice, also did an etching of the block, but it is uncertain which of the two American expatriates etched it first. Maurice Prendergast rendered several striking watercolors of the arches in his own unique post impressionist style in 1898–99. The scene has changed considerably from the nineteenth century. The quay now extends past the building and stretches to the public gardens. A broad paved walkway is in front of the buildings and a metal rail has replaced the stonework of the balcony on the right. No longer are boats pulled on the shore, no longer do lace-makers sit in the alleyways, but copious amounts of laundry still hang off the façades and down the long alleys beyond. ED

1. Kennedy 197, second state.

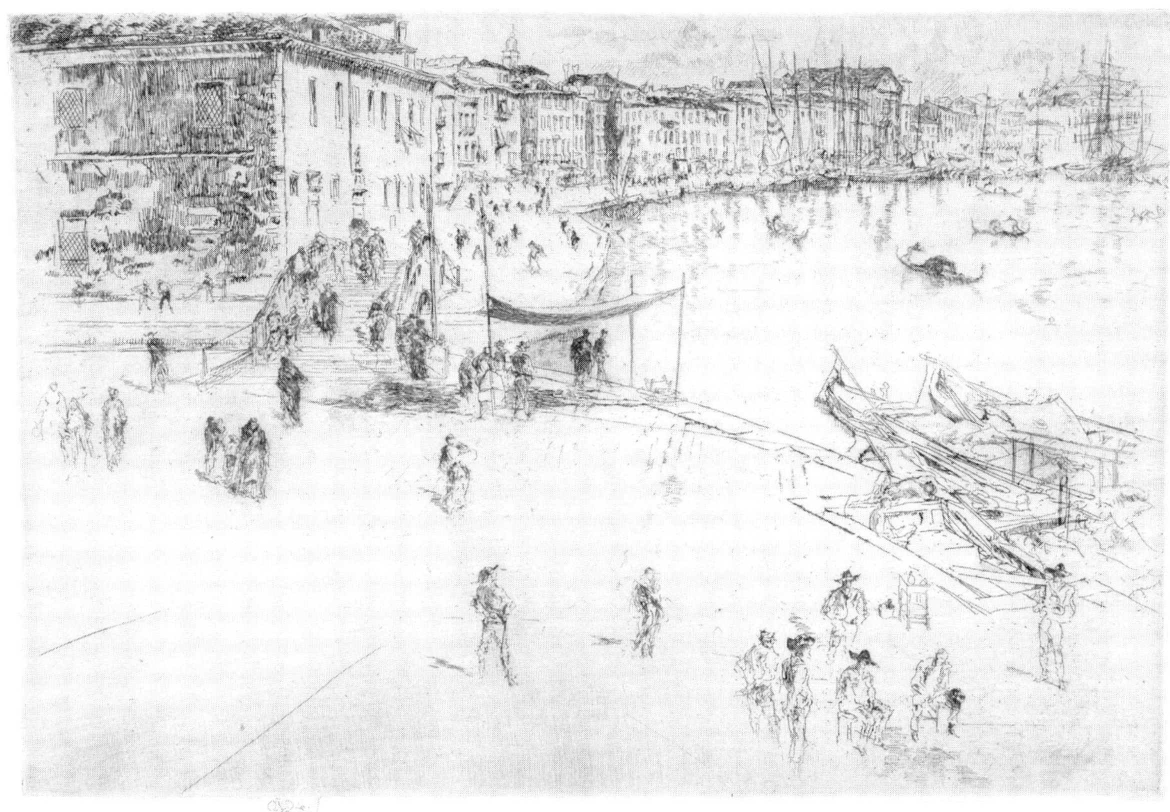

One of "Twenty-Six Etchings" (Second Venice Set)
Etching
Laid paper
Kennedy 206 ii/II; Mansfield 203
Signed, recto, upper left in plate: artist's monogram (butterfly);
lower left on tab, in graphite: artist's monogram (butterfly) and "imp."
Checklist 46

The Riva, No. 2, 1879-80

Whistler drew many images, both etchings and pastels, from the windows of the boarding house in which he lived during his final five months in Venice in summer and autumn 1880. Some he did from the southern side of the L-shaped Casa Jankowitz, looking across the lagoon to the island and Church of San Giorgio. Others looked west toward Piazza San Marco. *The Riva, No. 2*, and its variant *The Riva, No. 1* (CHECKLIST 39, ILLUS. P. 69), constitute the most elaborate of these views west along the wide Riva degli Schiavoni, stretching from Campo San Biagio to the domes of the basilica in San Marco.

Whistler worked from the second or third floor of the boarding house, and devoted the entire lower half of the composition to details of life in Campo San Biagio, including approximately two-dozen people walking or talking, standing or sitting. Whistler indicated the time of day, morning, by the direction of the shadows; the position of the boats suggests low tide. The right side of the composition is dominated by the expansive basin of San Marco, the calm waters disturbed only by the movement of a few gondolas. Along the left side of the etching a little more than halfway up the plate stands Ponte de l'Arsenal. At this point the riva rotates gently west, although Whistler emphasized a more dramatic angle. Beyond the bridge is the largest structure in the etching, the old arsenal military bakery, constructed in 1473 in a late Gothic style. This bakery produced the biscuits that supplied the Venetian maritime fleet. Whistler depicted the bakery with its east façade in shadow, an afternoon effect inconsistent with shadows in the foreground. The upper third of the etching comprises the rest of the riva, including a variety of hotels, rooming houses, and the prominent façade of the church of the Pieta, Santa Maria di Visitazione. Beyond that church at the end of the riva, largely obscured by sailing ships, are the Ducal Palace and the domes of the basilica. Whistler omitted the Campanile of San Marco in this image, although he had included a faint outline of it in the view he included in the First Venice Set.

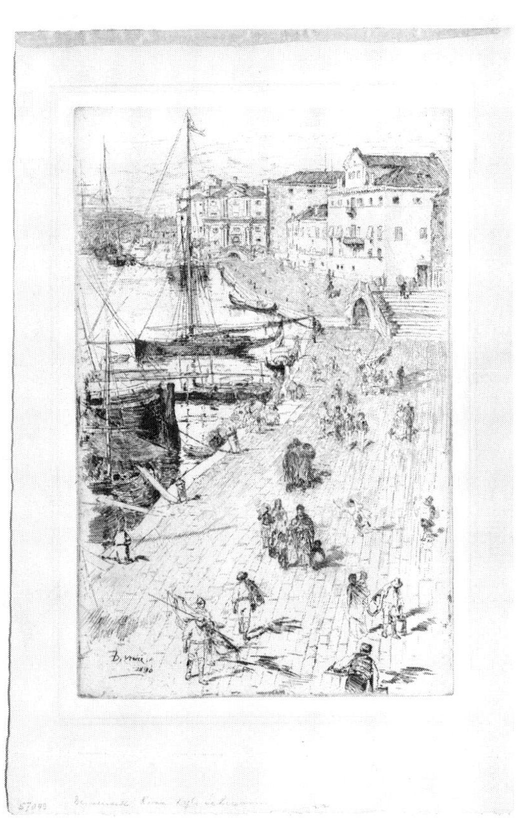

Riva degli Schiavoni II, 1880
Frank Duveneck
Etching on laid paper
sheet height: 13.66 in x 11.38 in wide
plate and image height: 13.15 in x 8.54 in wide
The Sterling and Francine Clark Art Institute, Williamstown, Massachusetts. Gift of Mrs. Helen Byrne Hackett Kelly.

According to Otto Bacher, Whistler adopted the compositional format for these views from the work of fellow American expatriate artist Frank Duveneck.[1] In *Riva degli Schiavoni, #1*, Duveneck represented the view from his balcony looking west in the direction of Piazza San Marco. He lived along Riva degli Schiavoni in Casa Kirsch, an inexpensive rooming house not far from the church of the Pieta, about halfway between Piazza San Marco and Whistler's rooms at Casa Jankowitz. Encouraged by one of his students, Otto Bacher, Duveneck had begun etching in Venice during the summer of 1880. His earliest views of Riva degli Schiavoni along the basin of San Marco, prompted Whistler to adopt this approach in both of his etchings of the riva. In turn, Whistler's earlier etched scenes encouraged Duveneck not to reverse the designs on the plate. Thus both men produced mirror images of the sites.

The two men's etchings otherwise stand in stark contrast. Duveneck chose a higher vantage point and employed a vertical format to stress the depth of the scene; Whistler's two images are horizontal, relaxing the sense of deep recession in Duveneck's prints. The strong diagonals in Duveneck's etching direct the eye to the prominent and identifiable Ducal Palace, an important and recognizable attraction to visitors. His heavily worked etching presents an abundance of anecdotal detail. Whistler's economical, more spacious compositions demonstrate a greater delicacy in the handling of details. Moreover Whistler's focal point, in contrast with Duveneck's, remains on a far less significant and anonymous structure: the architecturally unremarkable military bakery, with the broad swath of the riva only minimally detailed in front of it. A simple comparison between their handling of Campo San Biagio in the foreground attests to Whistler's greater sensitivity to open area of composition as opposed to a graphic horror vacui on the part of the younger artist. ED

1. Bacher, *With Whistler in Venice*, p. 144.

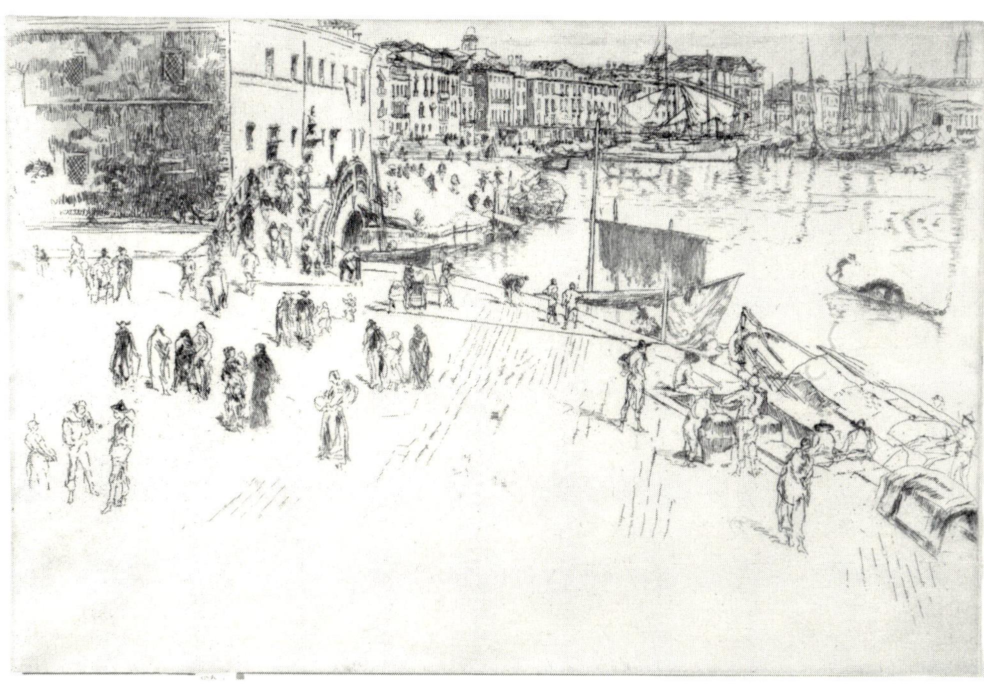

The Riva, No. 1 (Third State), 1879-80
Etching on laid paper
Gift of Jean K. Weil in memory of Adolph "Bucks" Weil, Jr.
1999.7.140

One of "Twenty-Six Etchings" (Second Venice Set)
Drypoint
Laid paper
Signed, recto, lower left on tab, in graphite: artist's monogram (butterfly) and "imp. 2nd proof"
Kennedy 203 ii/II; Mansfield 200
Checklist 45

Long Lagoon, 1879-80

CATALOGUE ENTRY 18

In *Long Lagoon*, Whistler employed one of his favorite approaches to Venice, a panoramic view across a broad stretch of the lagoon with a narrow strip of land placed on a remote horizon. The distant islands, with a few recognizable landmarks, were a thin foil for the expanse of water in the foreground and the extensive sky. More than a quarter of his Venetian etchings represented variations on this lyrical theme. Whistler accentuated the breadth of these subjects by composing a horizontal format: a few parallel ripples in the water, and a few thin clouds in the sky echo the long horizon line. He balanced the stress upon the horizontal composition by incorporating a small number of verticals: a bell tower or two, the masts of ships, bricole, the channel markers in the lagoon, and the reflections of all of these on the surface of the water. Through this economy of means the artist emphasized the fragile nature of the island city in contrast to the vast lagoon and infinite sky. The paintings and watercolors of the great British landscapist of the first half of the nineteenth century James M. W. Turner undoubtedly influenced Whistler's approach. For example, Turner's *Approach to Venice* (1844, National Gallery of Art, Washington, D.C.) represented a barely discernable view of the city with just a few domes and towers giving definition to the skyline of the islands in the distance.

Whistler drew many of these lagoon views from points along the quay of Riva degli Schiavoni, the walkway adjacent to the basin of San Marco extending from the Piazzetta to the Public Gardens. For *Long Lagoon* the artist went to the southernmost point of sestiere Castello: Punta della Motta, at the far end of the gardens. In the nineteenth century this was the end of the district. For the etching, Whistler faced west from Punta della Motta, across the lagoon to the southern part of the islands of La Giudecca. As usual, Whistler drew his design directly onto the grounded plate, resulting in the reversal of the image in the printing process.

The artist placed the horizon line slightly above the middle of the plate, with a few waves in the water below, and a few spare clouds above. Whistler gave no indication of his location, as was often the case—he might be standing on shore or moored in a gondola. In this way, Whistler's panoramic views parallel his treatment of facades across indeterminate expanses of water (see CAT. ENTRY 12, P. 55.) The Giudecca occupies the left part of the horizon, with the dome and campanile of Palladio's Church of the Redentore seen from behind. The mass of the church, and its reflection, are balanced by two three-masted sailing vessels on the right. Whistler depicted several bricole and gondolas toward the center of the etching that anchor the composition and provide a minimal sense of depth. *Long Lagoon* was included in the Second Venice Set, published by Dowdeswell & Dowdeswell gallery in 1886. The delicate impression in the MMFA was printed in dark brown ink from a plate that was carefully wiped, although the artist sometimes left a veil of ink on this etching to create additional atmosphere. ED

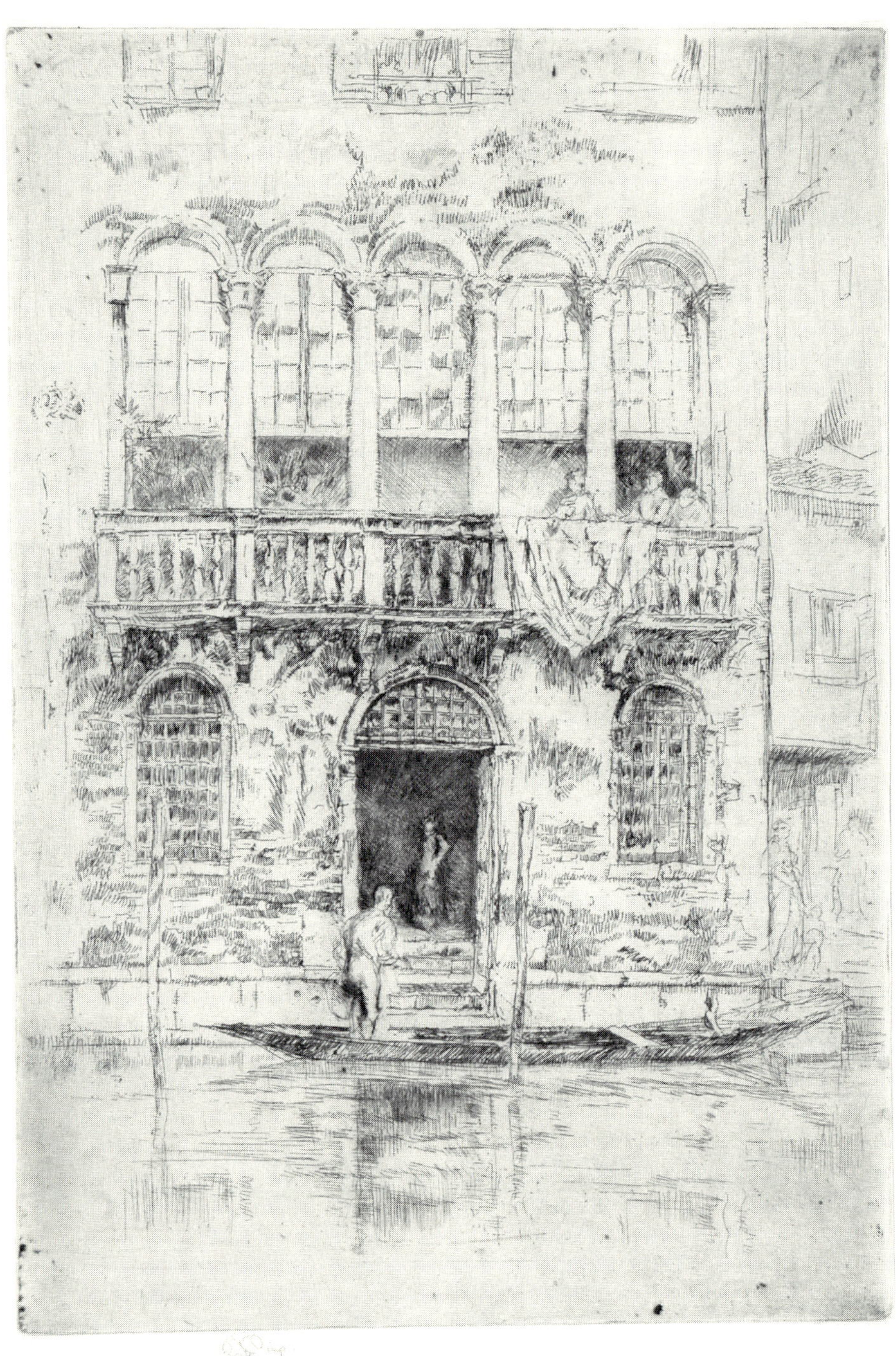

One of "Twenty-Six Etchings" (Second Venice Set)
Etching and drypoint
Laid paper
Signed, recto, upper left on plate: artist's monogram (butterfly); lower left on tab, in graphite: artist's monogram (butterfly)
and "imp."
Kennedy 207 iii/XI; Mansfield 204
Checklist 47

The Balcony, 1879-80

Whistler chose a site on Rio de San Pantalon at the end of an insignificant alley for *The Balcony*, a monumental Venetian etching. The canal demarcates sestiere Santa Croce from sestiere Dorsoduro. Whistler sat in Dorsoduro at the end of Calle dei Prete o del Pistor (street of the priests or the bakers), near the rear of Scuola Grande di San Rocco. He looked west across the canal to the Renaissance palace at number 66 Santa Croce. (Today Ponte del Vinanti spans the canal at this point, creating a thoroughfare that leads to the carpark at Piazzale Roma.)

The Balcony demonstrates Whistler's ability to creatively manipulate space. The artist again placed the viewer at a right angle, perpendicular to a palace from across an indeterminate expanse of water. A sandolo rides in the foreground, parallel to the façade. Different figures came and went from the boat, in the doorway, and on the balcony through the many different stages in the development of the print. The balcony spans the five arched windows on the second floor, the piano nobile (main public rooms) of the palace. On the level above, Whistler lightly sketched several windows; to the right he used faint lines to summarily indicate another building.

Whistler's primary interest lay in the balance and arrangement of windows and doors, of glass and grillwork, and of the arched windows and the balustrade. Whistler imbued the building with an unusual monumentality, showing it almost three stories high, from an impressive distance across a canal. The scale encouraged many researchers to assume the building lay along a major waterway, perhaps even the Grand Canal. In reality, the palace is relatively small and Rio di San Pantalon is relatively narrow, making both elements at complete odds with Whistler's presentation. Yet such extreme modification of space, and consequent reordering of scale, characterizes many of Whistler's Venetian prints. By starting in the center of the sheet and working outward (see CAT. ENTRY 12, P. 55) Whistler freely revised the conventional delineations of pictorial space. Most of his compositions rendered the indispensable features of the central motif, whether a distant view of Venice shimmering on the lagoon, a close up image of an archway leading to a murky canal, or a view of a doorway in a waterside façade.

Whistler's contemporary, John Singer Sargent, and later John Marin both worked in this immediate area. Sargent executed a series of watercolors of the back of Scuola Grande di San Rocco just north of this palace at the intersection Rio de San Pantalon, Rio de la Muneghete, and Rio de la Frescada. In 1907 Marin drew *From the Ponte S. Pantaleo, Venice*, an etching that included a side view of the same palace that Whistler depicted in *The Balcony*.

The MMFA's *The Balcony* is an extremely rare impression of an early trial stage in the development of the composition. It may be the image reproduced in the Kennedy catalogue raisonné as state III, which in 1909 belonged to the Royal Library.[1] ED

1. Kennedy 207, belonging to Bibliotheque Royale de Windsor, London.

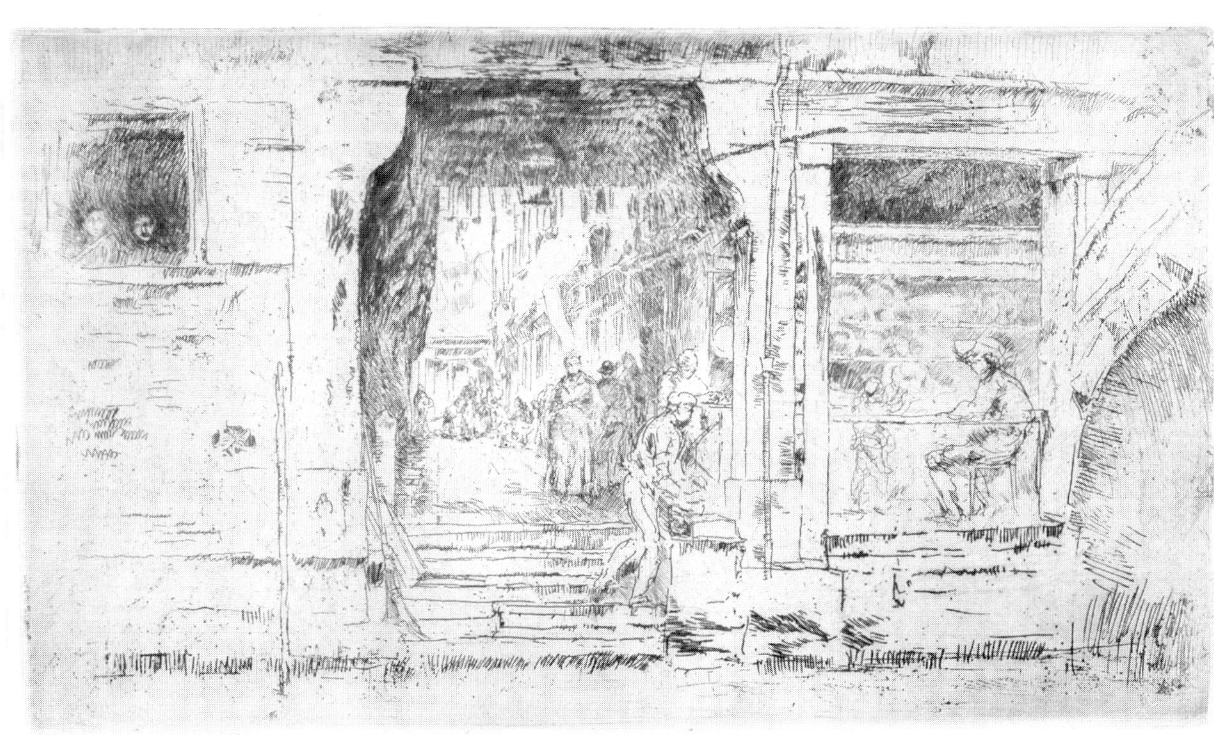

Etching
Laid paper
Signed, recto, center left in plate: artist's monogram (butterfly)
Kennedy 218 v/VII; Mansfield 215
Checklist 50

Fish-Shop, Venice, 1879-80

CATALOGUE ENTRY 20

The site of *Fish-Shop, Venice* is in sestiere San Marco, not far off the merceria, the major commercial passageway that leads from Piazza San Marco to the Rialto bridge.[1] After crossing Ponte dei Bareteri heading west, the underpass adjacent to the bridge leads north to another underpass, the portico at the end of Calle de le Acque. Whistler viewed the scene from a building opposite the entrance to the portico, accessible by Ponte de le Acque, partially included on the right side of the etching. The etching is a mirror image of the actual site.

Fish-Shop, Venice is one of a small number of Venetian prints that Whistler excluded from both Venice sets. The reason for the omission remains unclear. The view is typical of Whistler's approach to canal-side façades, looking across the waterway from a position perpendicular to the plane of the buildings; the façade is cropped on the sides and the top, and in the center of the plate is a shadowed opening into an illuminated space in the distance. However, Whistler treated a number of the formal elements differently. He left few open areas on the copper plate in the passages that are clearly peripheral to the central motif. He expended a good deal of effort on the shadows beneath the bridge and the underpass on the right side. The window on the left he carefully detailed with several prominent heads. The strip of water in the foreground is minimal—probably at low tide given Whistler's description of the steps opposite. The composition appears busier and more finished than those for similar subjects, for example *The Doorway* (CAT. ENTRY 12, P. 55) or *The Balcony* (CAT. ENTRY 19, P. 73). His explanation to Mortimer Menpes of the secret of composition (see p. 55) does not apply to this print, which raises the possibility that Whistler executed this plate early in the Venetian trip, before achieving his aesthetic epiphany.

Whistler worked the surface of the plate in a variety of ways to create a rich tapestry of effects. The shadow beneath the bridge is broadly sketched, contrasting with the careful line work that establishes the shadows around the seated figure on the right. The deep shadows of the passageway are heavily crosshatched and bitten, contrasting with the light on the alley way beyond and the third underpass seen in the distance. A few parallel lines are sufficient to create the Istrian stone of the steps, and just a few marks on the plate convey the mortar of the wall on the left.

The MMFA impression of *Fish-Shop, Venice* is from an intermediate stage in the development of the image. Although Whistler often selectively wiped the narrow register of water in the foreground, he cleanly wiped this proof so that the etched lines created both tone and surface interest.

The maze of streets and canals in this area of San Marco attracted many artists looking for characteristic views of the city in the wake of Whistler's new approach. Just north of the setting of *Fish-Shop, Venice*, this canal intersects with Rio della Fava. Around the corner to the west, on Riva Tonda, John Marin sat and drew *Rio della Fava, Venezia*, a view of the abrupt turn in the canal. John Singer Sargent sat in a gondola adjacent to the spot, sketching a watercolor in the opposite direction of the watergate entrance to Palazzo Giustiniani-Faccanon. Both American artists were about fifty yards from where Whistler had done his image of Palazzo Gussoni, *The Doorway*, on the same canal. ED

1. Grieves, *Whistler's Venice*, pp. 95–96.

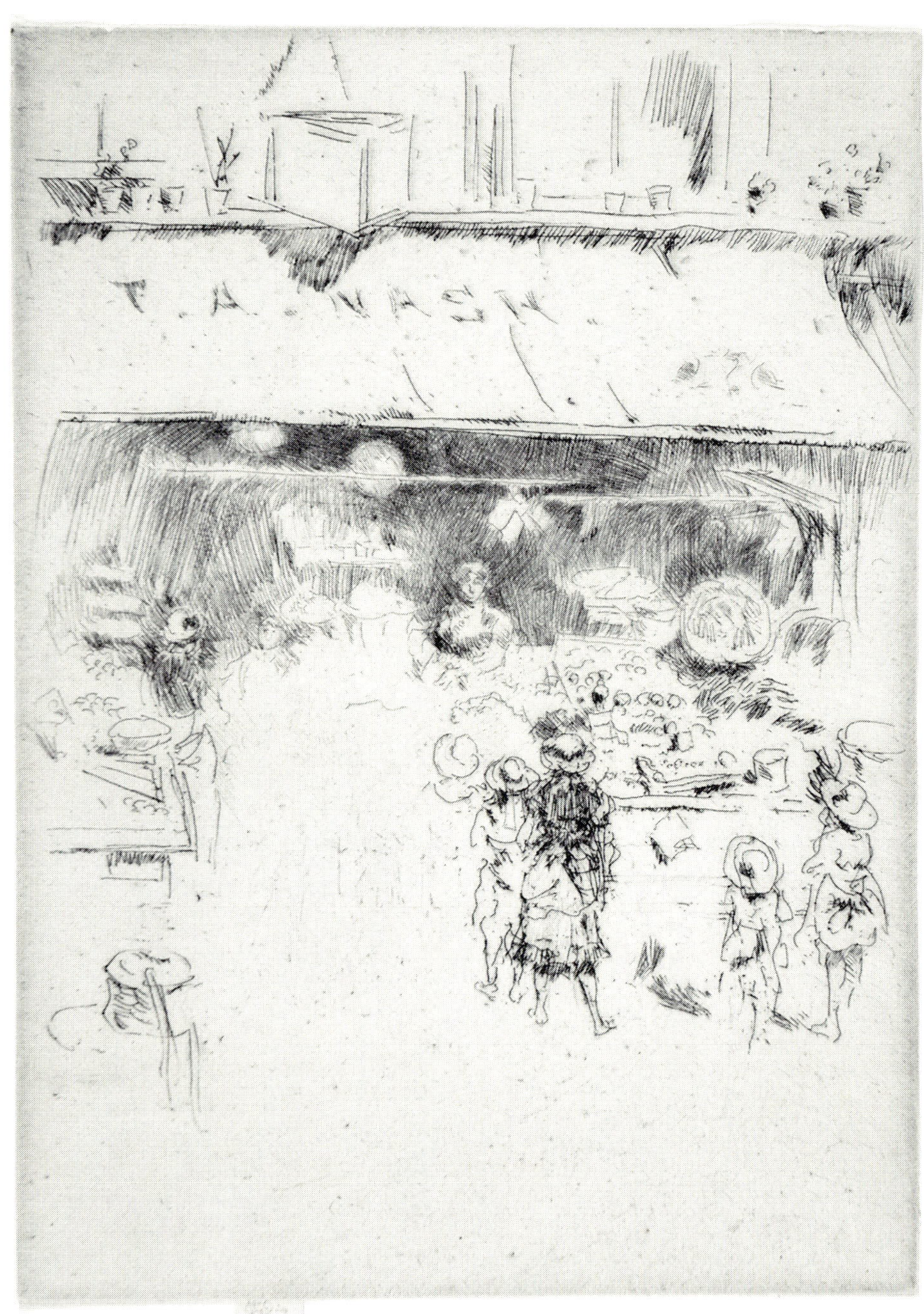

Etching
Japanese paper
Signed, recto upper right in plate: artist's monogram (butterfly); and lower left on sheet in graphite: artist's monogram (butterfly) and "imp."
Kennedy 263 iv/IV; Mansfield 260
Checklist 52

T.A. Nash's Fruit-Shop, ca. 1886

CATALOGUE ENTRY 21

After Whistler returned to London in 1881, he revisited the subject of English urban life, continuing his earlier explorations of the city and taking his inspirations from the works of French art critic Charles Baudelaire and French cartoonist Paul Gavarni. In London, as in Paris in the 1850s, Whistler made regular trips into picturesque districts in search of realist subjects. At this time, Whistler began to construct his images of London in a more abstract manner than he had previously. His use of broad areas of open space, his interest in symmetry, and his contrasts of light and shadow represent a stylistic shift in the new work, clearly evident in *T.A. Nash's Fruit-Shop.*

Whistler's students, Walter Sickert and Mortimer Menpes in particular, accompanied the artist as he sought places that would make compelling compositions of contemporary life. By this point in his career Whistler viewed drawing on plates as sketching, commencing many plates in the presence of the motif that were then finished later in his studio.

The artist produced a series of approximately sixty plates from 1880 to 1887. They depict shops, building façades, and London streetscapes. Whistler referred to these collectively as the "Little London" set, but it was never published. As a whole the works present flat façades containing strong architectural elements, sparse lines and brief suggestions of people. *T.A. Nash's Fruit-Shop*, a detailed and balanced composition, depicts a group of women and children shopping at a local London fruit shop. Within a letter to Charles Dowdeswell, director of the Dowdeswell and Dowdeswell gallery in London, written in September of 1887 or 1888, Whistler listed the etching under the title "Little London."

Throughout the etching Whistler manipulated the scene by darkening and finishing the details in the areas of greatest interest: the face of the shop keeper emerges from the dark shadows of the stall; rows and rows of fruit capture the attention of the children. He gave subordinate objects and characters a sketchier, summary treatment. The symmetry and balance within the composition are key elements in Whistler's later etchings. The shadows, figures, and detail complement and contrast with each other. Dark, heavily worked areas counter the light areas of untouched paper. The flowerpots and the windows above the shop frame the composition and echo the foreground details. By restricting the focus of the scene and creating visual frames with the architectural elements Whistler allowed a two-dimensional pattern to emerge.

Whistler evoked a sense of beauty through the design of the composition and the harmony of the lines. He was concerned with theories of finish and proportion in his art, both in painting and printmaking during the 1880s. In 1886, in a publication entitled *Propositions*, Whistler articulated his theoretical position on etching and in the process denounced the then popular large etching plates and supported and defended less formal, more intimate works that allowed viewers to appreciate symmetry and harmony.[1]

> That in Art, it is criminal to go beyond the means used in its exercise.
>
> That the space to be covered should always be in proper relations to the means used for covering it.
>
> That in etching, the means used, or instrument employed, being the smallest possible point, the space to be covered should be small in proportion.
>
> That all attempts to overstep the limits insisted upon by such proportion, are inartistic thoroughly, and tend to reveal the paucity of the means used, instead of concealing the same, as required by Art in its refinement.
>
> That the huge plate, therefore, is an offence—its undertaking an unbecoming display of determination and ignorance—its accomplishment a triumph of unthinking earnestness and uncontrolled energy—endowments of the "duffer."

That the custom of "Remarque" emanates from the amateur, and reflects his foolish facility beyond the border of his picture, thus testifying to his unscientific sense of its dignity.

That it is odious.

That, indeed, there should be no margin on the proof to receive such "Remarque"

That the habit of margin, again, dates from the outsider, and continues with the collector in his unreasoning connoisseurship—taking curious pleasure in the quantity of the paper.

That the picture ending where the frame begins, and in the case of the etching, the white mount, being inevitably, because of its colour, the frame, the picture this extends itself irrelevantly through the margin to the mount.

That wit of this kind should leave six inches of raw canvas between the painting and its gold frame, to delight the purchaser with the quality of the cloth.

Whistler printed four different states of this etched plate. The differences between the first and the fourth states lie in the deepening of the shadows. JWR

1. Reprinted in Whistler, *The Gentle Art of Making Enemies*, p 76.

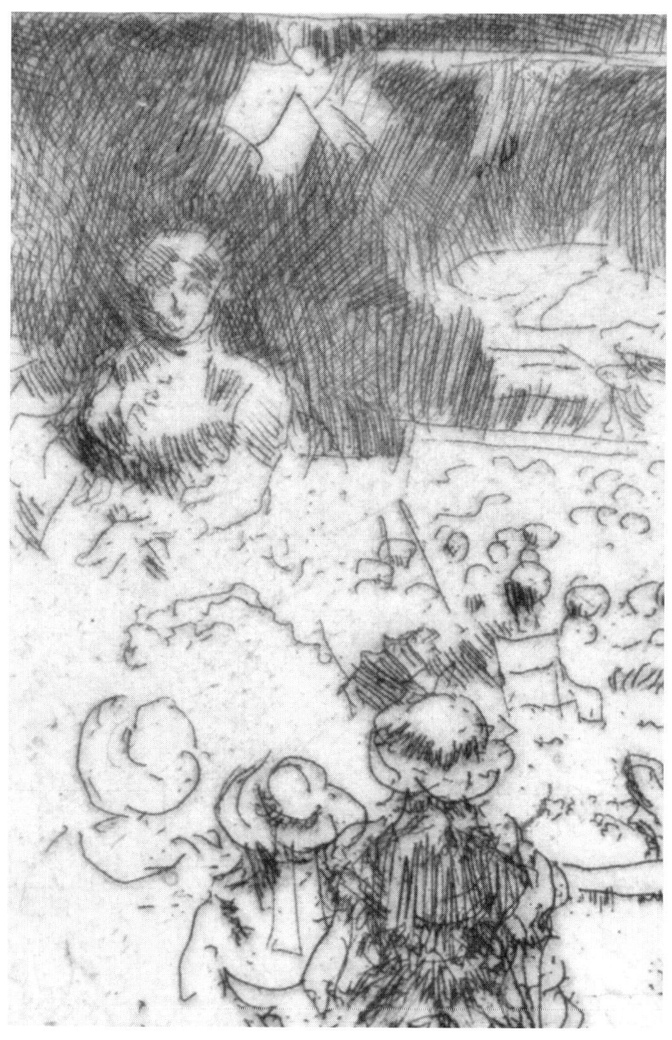

Detail from *T. A. Nash's Fruit Shop* (Fourth State), 1886
Etching on Japanese paper
Gift of Mr. and Mrs. Adolph Weil, Jr., in memory of Mr. and Mrs. Adolph Weil, Sr.
1992.2.14

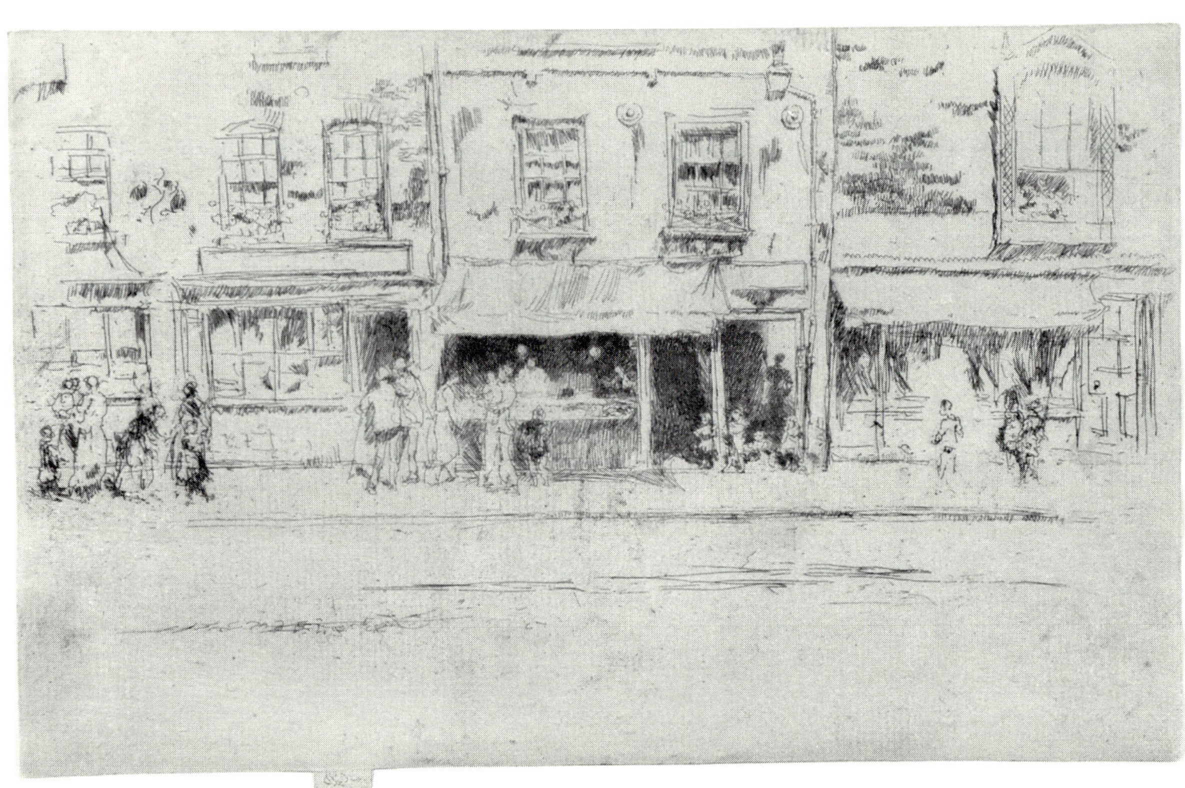

Etching
Laid paper
Signed, recto, upper left in plate: artist's monogram (butterfly);
lower left on tab, in graphite: artist's monogram (butterfly) and "imp."
Kennedy 264 i/II; Mansfield 259
Checklist 53

The Fish-Shop, Busy Chelsea, ca. 1884-86 CATALOGUE ENTRY 22

Whistler favored shop fronts and façades involving series of projecting awnings and receding doorways as subjects for etchings in the 1880s. Mortimer Menpes, a student of Whistler's, later recreated the scene of a typical day during which the two artists ventured through the streets of London searching for an appropriate subject:

> Then Whistler would get out his little pochade box, and together we would drift out into the open,—on to the Embankment, or down a side street in Chelsea,—and he would make a little sketch, sometimes in water, sometimes in oil colour. It might be a fish shop with eels for sale at so much a plate, and a few soiled children in the foreground; or perhaps a sweet-stuff shop, and the children standing with their faces glued to the pane. There we would stay and paint until luncheon time, sitting on rush-bottomed chairs borrowed from the nearest shop. Wherever Whistler went he caused interest and excitement: men, women, and children flocked about him—especially children, Chelsea children, shoals of them. [1]

The Fish-Shop, Busy Chelsea figures among his most ambitious London street scenes. Until 1900 Elizabeth Maunder's fish shop was located at 72 Cheyne Walk, not far from Whistler's home, and was the subject of several of Whistler's prints and an oil painting. Whistler revealed an intimate and picturesque scene of daily life in Chelsea in this etching and expended great care in the compositional arrangement.

The Fish-Shop, Busy Chelsea holds a distinctive place within Whistler's most powerful etchings because of its design. Within a tiny plate Whistler created a rich architectural façade by implementing a calligraphic line and an intricate balance of shade and light. The fish shop stands in center of the etching, framed by adjoining storefronts. Its receding dark shades contrast with the closed windows and doors of the adjoining shops. The first-floor windows echo the patterning of flat and receding spaces. In combination these elements focus attention on the central dark shadows.

In the scene men, women and children actively fulfill or ignore daily chores. The people and their actions become part of the streetscape, owing to Whistler's integration of the figures with the patterns of the shadows, and add to the illusion of depth and space. The shopkeeper emerges from the dark background underneath the awning. To the right of the fish shop a doorway is framed by a group of children, a silhouette of a figure emphasized against the light. Close examination of the etching reveals details of costume and of the figures and their proximity to one another, but no singular narrative is apparent.

Whistler signed the work on the upper left corner with his trademark butterfly signature. The positioning of the butterfly signature within the etching appears as a decorative architectural detail. It emphasized Whistler's beliefs that an artist has the right to pick and choose among the elements of nature to create a beautiful scene and that nature does not provide balanced and harmonious artistic compositions. Whistler created this harmonious design by selecting, comparing, and contrasting elements derived from observation and rendering them in intricate decorative patterns.

JWR

1. Menpes, *Whistler as I Knew Him*, p. 3.

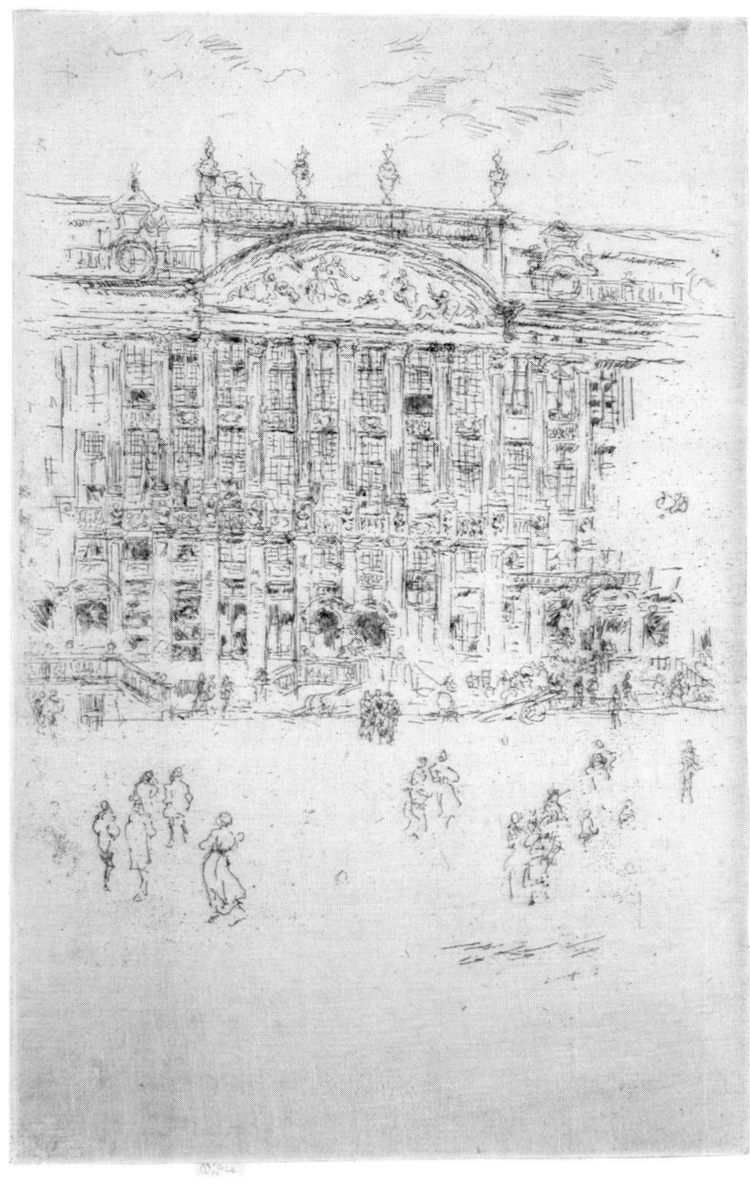

Etching
Laid paper
Signed, recto, center right in plate: artist's monogram (butterfly);
lower left on tab, in graphite: artist's monogram (butterfly) and "imp."
Kennedy 362 only state; Mansfield 354
Checklist 54

Grand' Place, Brussels, 1887

CATALOGUE ENTRY 23

Grand' Place, Brussels, a relatively late etching in the course of Whistler's printmaking career, provides an interesting milepost in his artistic development. He created it during a period of positive attention for his work and when he had achieved a new level of financial stability. Whistler drew the image on a journey to Holland and Belgium in the autumn of 1887 with Dr. William and Helen Whistler, his brother and sister-in-law. Travel often inspired Whistler, and the trip was no exception; it resulted in nineteen etchings, thirteen of which depict Belgium. [1]

In this etching, Whistler chose to depict the wide plaza that leads up to the façade of a monumental structure. The Grand' Place is the tourist center of Brussels, a vast city square surrounded by immense seventeenth-century guild houses and government buildings. For his image, Whistler framed the center portion of the Hotel des Ducs de Brabant, built in 1696–98 by Guillame de Bruyn, the architect who coordinated the rebuilding of much of the city after the French bombardment of 1695. [2]

In the composition Whistler focused on the structure of the building and the surrounding urban space. He reduced the figures to summary indications in the foreground, placing them to provide a sense of scale to the viewer. His interest in the arrangement of architectural detail and ornament harkened back to a number of the Venetian etchings of 1879–80. Like several of those he began the composition with one detail at the center of the image and worked out towards the edges, allowing the detail to gently fade off as the etching needle moved further away from the important central motif.[3] Whistler used his most substantial line work to describe the central elements of the façade; the lines became less and less significant as he rendered the ancillary details of the composition. To convey the play of light and shadow over the façade he varied concentrations of lines and tones, and enhanced this by reducing the ornamentation to only the essential lines. He pushed his economic use of line so far that the image seems to float in the middle of the page. The extreme reduction of expressive means lent itself to a reduction of stability and form in the composition, an effect which pleased Whistler who was excited to have his etching approximate the visual nature of a piece of lace.

Notorious for avoiding popular tourist views as the subjects of his etchings, Whistler's decision to depict a well-known, recognizable landmark in Brussels' most famous plaza remains perplexing. Possibly Whistler was consciously playing with the very idea of recognition. Perhaps the novelty of his approach to both technique and printing emboldened him to suggest that he could select a well-known site and obtain a new and unrecognizable view to the public. In any case, *Grand' Place, Brussels* is informed by a delicacy and lightness that is most characteristic of his work in this late period. EKJ

1. Lochnan, *Etchings of James McNeill Whistler*, p. 240.
2. *La patrimonie monumental de la Belgique: Bruxelles*, p. 150.
3. Lochnan, *Etchings of James McNeill Whistler*, p. 241.

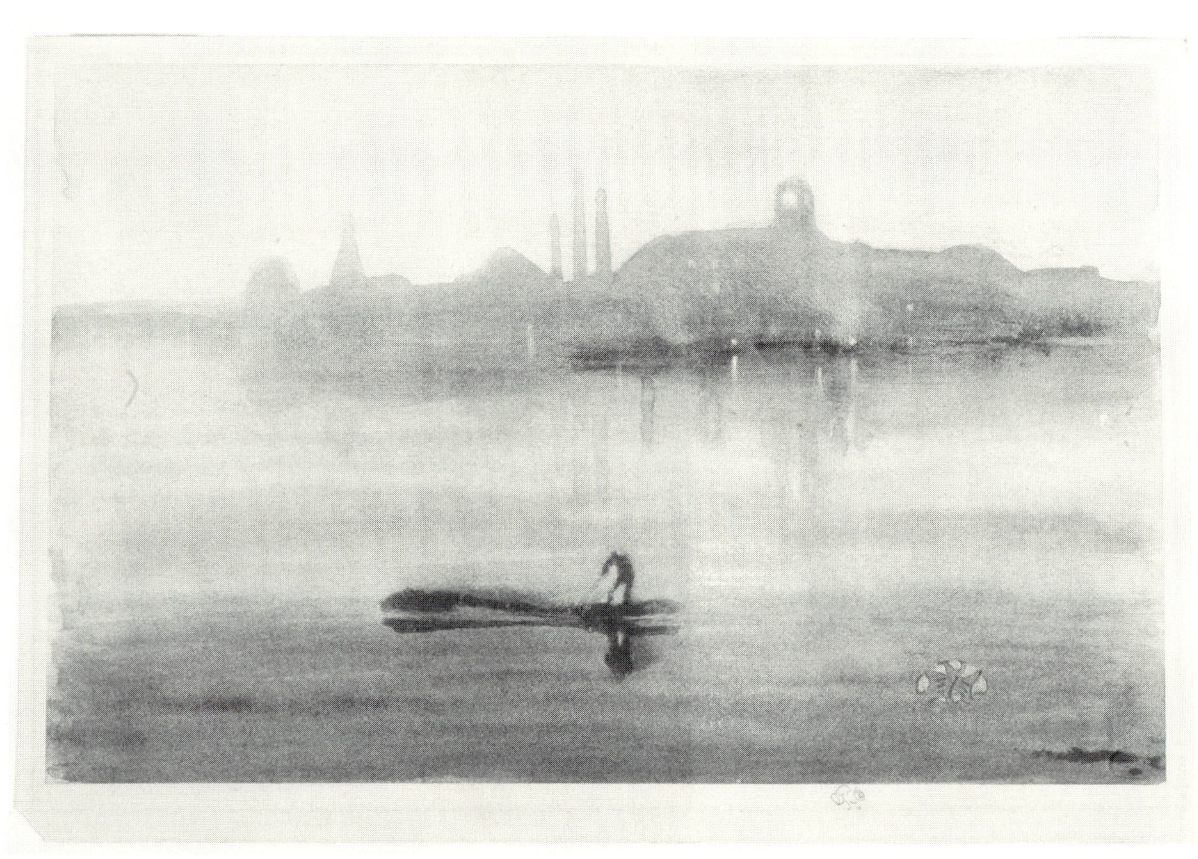

Lithotint
Wove proofing paper
Signed, recto, lower right in plate: artist's monogram (butterfly); lower right in graphite: artist's monogram (butterfly)
Chicago 8 1/2; Way 5; Levy 10; proof state, not published
Checklist 57

Nocturne, 1878

In 1878 and 1879 printer Thomas Way persuaded Whistler to experiment with lithography. The artist's earliest attempts in the medium, not including his student years at West Point, produced twenty prints. His interest occurred at a time of financial difficulty as a result of his loss of patronage stemming from his public disputes with his patron Fredrick Leyland's commission for the Peacock room, and at the height of his famous libel suit against art critic John Ruskin. Soon after the conclusion of that trial Whistler abandoned lithography for about a decade.

Whistler completed *Nocturne*, a view of the river at Battersea, in 1878. Throughout the 1870s, Whistler had devoted his painting to powerful aesthetic compositions inspired by evening mists and night scenes of the Thames and the adjacent riverbanks. While still engaged by aspects of the modern city for his subjects, he broke from his earlier work that depicted daylight scenes of industrial areas to suggest the veils of fog and the shadows of night on the river. He produced at least thirty-two oil paintings with this approach, and this is his most similar print of the same period. The subject was the river he interacted with daily after moving to Chelsea in December of 1862. Whistler had repeatedly painted Battersea, an industrial area directly across the river from the borough of Chelsea, under a variety of lighting and atmospheric conditions since 1859. The lithotint reversed the Battersea shoreline during the printing process, but the distinguishing industrial landmarks remain readily identifiable: the spire of Battersea church, a silhouette of the plumbago works, the clock tower of Morgan Crucible Company (popularly known as "Mr. Ted Morgan's Folly"), and a series of warehouse chimneys.

Thomas Way watched Whistler work on this lithotint and later recalled that the artist's composition was "drawn in the dark, by feeling not sight." [1] Whistler, before beginning it, commented, "Now let us see if we can remember a Nocturne." [2]

Initially, Whistler referred to his nighttime scenes of the river as "moonlights." Patron Frederick Leyland, suggested the term "nocturne," which Whistler embraced because of its link to a form of abstraction that he connected to music. In his defining spoken and published description of his aesthetic approach, *Ten O'Clock* (originally delivered as a lecture in 1885), Whistler described his connection to and admiration for the beauty of the Thames.

> And when the evening mist clothes the riverside with poetry, as with a veil, and the poor buildings lose themselves in the dim sky and the tall chimneys become campanili, and the warehouses are palaces of the night and the whole city hangs in the heavens... and Nature, who for once, has sung in tune, sings her exquisite song to the artist alone. [3]

The same aesthetic sensibility infuses *Nocturne*. The print is a lithotint, a medium utilizing washes of ink, employed by the artist to produce a controlled tonal effect. Whistler applied the washes directly onto a lithographic stone prepared by Thomas Way and his son, Thomas R. Way. He highlighted certain passages of the design by brushing acid on the stone, adding accents with crayon, and scratching with a razor through the crayon. After the wash dried, Whistler scratched the surface of the stone to create lights throughout the composition. He achieved a remarkable range of atmospheric effects. He softened the lines of his drawing and created a hazy, atmospheric effect around the harsh industrial landscape. The blotting on the tops of the warehouses and smokestacks allowed them to disappear into the thick mist. In the foreground, the barge, the figures, and the ripples in the water are vividly rendered in color and texture.

Whistler's choice of paper also affected the distinctions of tone. Frequently Whistler experimented with a variety of different papers for each of his prints. Most proof impressions of the first state of *Nocturne* he printed on ivory or off-white paper. He introduced subtle changes to the image in the second state, and often chose to print on a pale-blue laid paper, which Way described as "grey-tinted paper mounted upon larger sheets of French plate-paper," and the evenly distributed blue fibers gave a completely different quality to the tones. JWR

1. Way & Dennis, *Memories of James McNeill Whistler*, p. 14.
2. Thomas R. Way, "Whistler's Lithographs," *Print Collector's Quarterly 3* (1911): 286.
3. James McNeill Whistler, *Ten O'Clock* (Boston: Houghton Mifflin, 1888), p. 20.

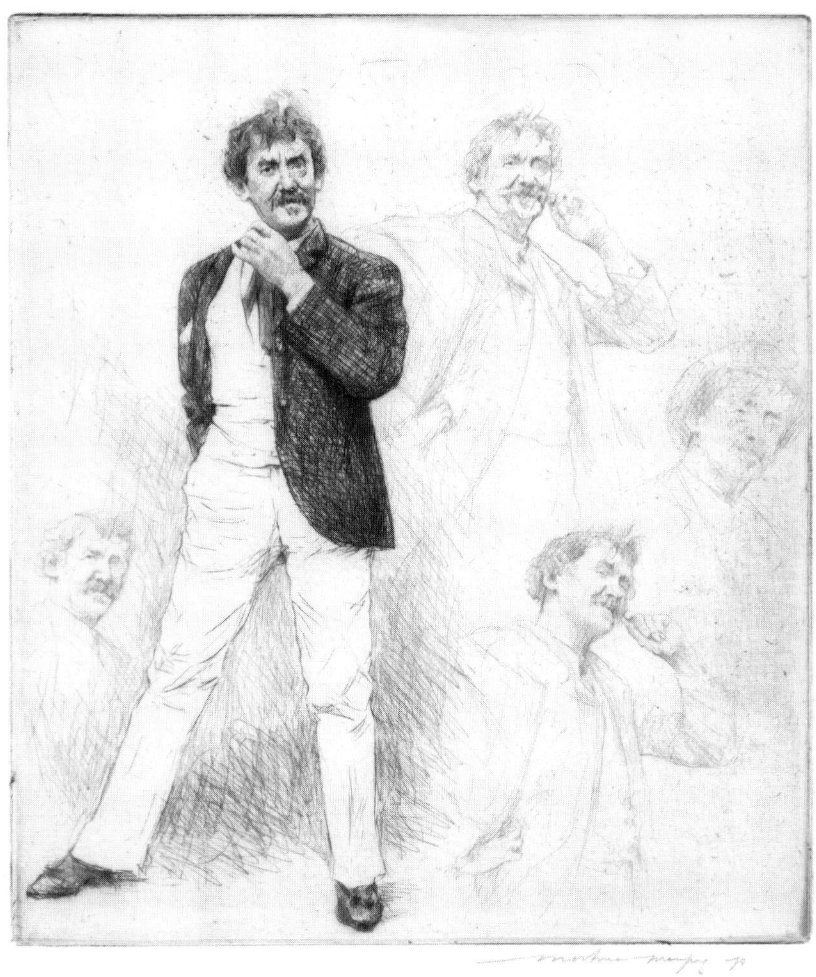

The Five Faces of Whistler (or *White Ducks*), c. 1890
Mortimer Menpes (Australian, 1855–1938)
Etching on paper
The Trout Gallery, Dickinson College, Carlisle, Pennsylvania.

Menpes moved from his native Australia to London in 1875, and after 1880 he began to study art informally with Whistler. He became a well-respected and exhibiting etcher and watercolorist in his own right, publishing a sizeable number of books illustrating people and places he experienced in his travels around the world during the first two decades of the twentieth century. In 1904, he wrote a memoir of Whistler titled Whistler as I Knew Him.

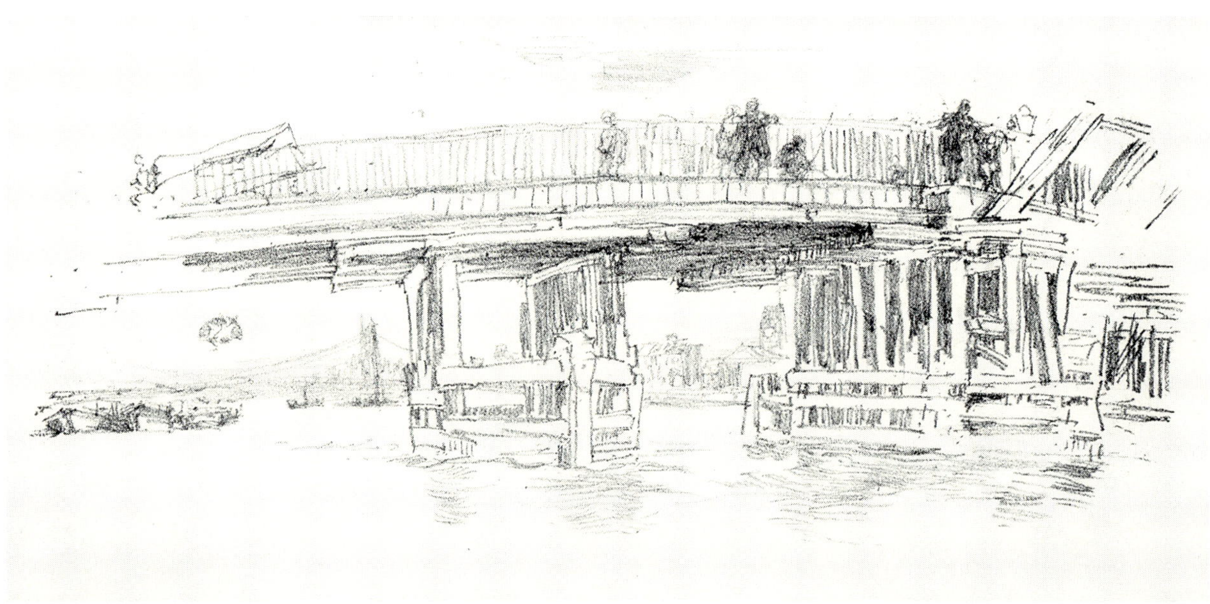

Lithograph
Laid paper
Signed, recto, left center in plate: artist's monogram (butterfly);
lower left in graphite: artist's monogram (butterfly)
Chicago 18 2/2; Way 12; Levy 24
Checklist 58

Old Battersea Bridge, 1879

CATALOGUE ENTRY 25

Lithography was a new medium for Whistler in 1878 and 1879, and it is somewhat striking that he should take up a relatively unfamiliar technique at an unstable and challenging point in his career. During these years, Whistler lost the patronage of his great benefactor, Frederic Leyland, brought a libel suit against John Ruskin, a notable art critic, and declared bankruptcy.

These summary details of Whistler's personal circumstances provide one explanation for his movement into lithography. Possibly Whistler also became interested in the medium as a means to reproduce images of his paintings cheaply and in large number. Lithography could produce larger numbers of good impressions more easily than Whistler's more familiar technique of etching. At the time other craftsmen had already produced a number of lithographs of Whistler's paintings, but these he had considered of unacceptably low standard. For what ever the reasons, Whistler became curious about the expressive possibilities of lithography in the late 1870s and began experimenting to see what effects he could achieve with the planographic medium.

During the previous two decades, many French artists had begun working in lithography, including Felix Bracquemond, Alphonse Legros, Edouard Manet, and Camille Pissarro, initiating a lithographic revival in France.[1] Whistler, a friend and colleague of this generation of French avant-garde artists, knew of their output. Furthermore, London-based printer Thomas Way, at times a catalyst, a cheerleader, and a supplier of materials, also encouraged Whistler in his investigations of lithography. Way believed in the artistic merits of the medium and provided the logistical support to enable the artist to explore lithography's unique versatility in drawing with both strong and subtle elements, in both sharp lines and soft, in both line and tone.

Whistler drew this image directly onto the lithographic stone while sitting in a boat on the Thames during high tide.[2] He rendered the scene with a notable immediacy, drawing the bridge from below, capturing the architectural solidity of the bridge's structure, the massed boats in the river beyond the bridge, and the development along the riverbank. Atop the bridge most pedestrians go about their daily lives, but a few have stopped, apparently to watch the artist at work. Whistler barely suggested the figures, provided the faintest outlines of buildings and boats, and allowed the structure of the bridge to fade into obscurity across the composition. The solid pier of the bridge is the single clearly delineated part of the design, and delicate ripples at the base suggestively indicate the waves of the Thames.

Although Whistler pulled a few impressions of *Old Battersea Bridge* in 1879, more were printed, with some minimal changes, in the portfolio Notes, published by Boussod, Valadon and Co. in 1887. Thomas Way claimed one hundred impressions of the lithograph between the two states, an assertion unsupported by other evidence. It is likely that the stone was erased by 1896.

The MMFA's impression comes from the estate of Rosalind Birnie Philip. She was the sister of Whistler's late wife Beatrice and became the executor of the artist's estate upon his death. This lithograph was in his studio at the time of his death in 1903. EKJ

1. Stratis & Tedeschi, *Lithographs of James McNeill Whistler*, p. 41.
2. Ibid., p. 96.
3. Ibid., 98.

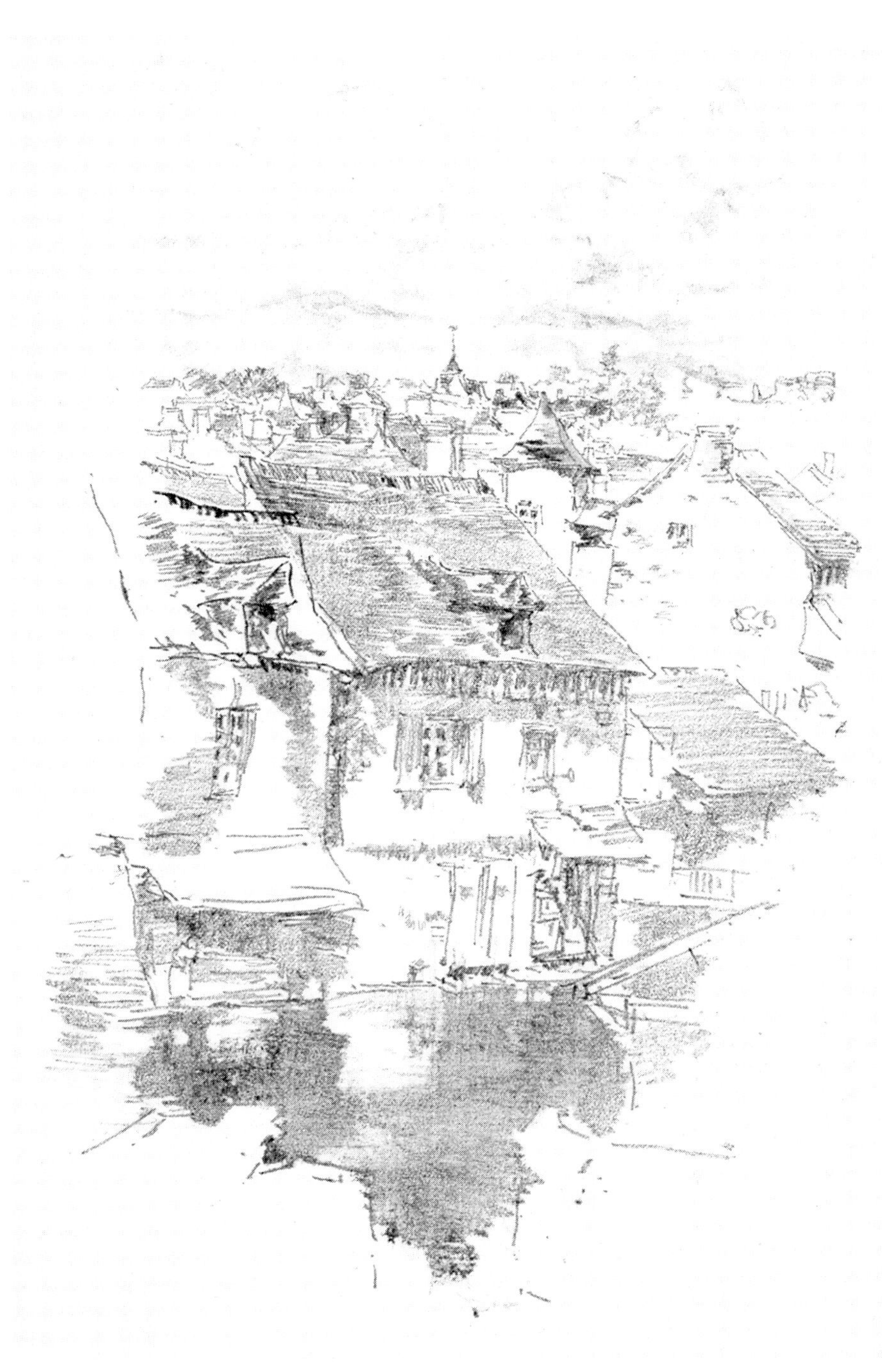

Lithograph
Laid paper
Signed, recto, center right in plate: artist's monogram (butterfly)
Chicago 63 only state; Way 39; Levy 65
Checklist 59

Vitré: The Canal, 1893

Whistler completed seventeen lithographs before he left for Venice in 1879, and he did not return to the medium until 1887. In 1888, Whistler married Beatrice Godwin, widow of his friend architect E. W. Godwin, who had designed the artist's White House and studio on Tite Street. Trixie, as she was known, encouraged Whistler to return to his earlier experiments with the medium. This marked the beginning of a period, when Whistler devoted himself to lithography. It remained his primary printmaking interest until Trixie's death in 1896.

In the late 1870s Whistler had drawn his images directly on the lithographic stones. When he returned to the medium in the late 1880s, he altered his technique and predominantly worked on lithographic transfer paper. The shift relieved him of the burden of carting the heavy lithographic stone and allowed him to sketch in open air, giving him greater freedom of movement. The liberty afforded by the transfer paper also allowed Whistler to send work easily from abroad. When Whistler and his wife moved to Paris in 1892, where they lived intermittently for the next three years, the advent of waxy lithographic transfer paper permitted the artist to draw sketches in Paris and send them to his printers Thomas Way and his son Thomas R. Way in London. When he mailed the sketches of *Vitré: The Canal*, Whistler sent specific instructions, as Way recalled later:

> [I received a drawing made with] chalk and finished with stump, the sky and watery foreground being almost entirely so drawn. Now, if this had been drawn upon stone, it would have been a simple matter for the printer; but it was done on transfer paper, and was new, and one dared not risk such a charming drawing without learning how to treat it. So I made some little drawings in the same manner, and had them put on stone, and worked out the proper treatment, and I was well rewarded by the successful result when the Canal was proved, and the confidence it gave him to follow this line of work with the perfect little group of lithographs of Luxembourg Gardens and The Nude Model Reclining. [1]

Vitré: The Canal marked the first time Whistler used a stump suffused with greasy crayon. The stump, a roll of paper, is used in lithography to soften the contours of the line and to create tonal values without markings. Way's account makes it clear that he was surprised that Whistler had employed the stump technique on transfer paper. Most artists used it directly on a stone.

Using the stump on the paper enabled Whistler to create a variety of atmospheric effects, depending on the amount of ink applied. The lines of *Vitré: The Canal* are heavier than in the majority of Whistler's previous lithographs. The Ways dampened the paper when the image was printed, and this also affected the final result. Painterly effects are evident throughout *Vitré: The Canal*. On September 20, 1893, Whistler wrote to Thomas R. Way:

> My Dear Tom. Just a line in great haste to tell you that I am delighted with the proofs—I don't want anything done to them—They are most delicate and beautifully printed—The stump skies I think quite charming and quite enough. There is a delightful velvety quality about them—and I just want at once to print out all the paper I have sent with these proofs—divided among them. [2]

In the spring of 1892, Whistler and Trixie moved to 110 rue du Bac in Paris. He undertook *Vitré: The Canal* and six other lithographs when they traveled to Brittany for a holiday in July and August 1893, and of these he sent five to Way. The subject of *Vitré: The Canal* is a group of houses along a canal in the old Breton town of Vitré. Whistler chose an elevated viewpoint overlooking the buildings. Across the canal and behind the houses, roof tops and towers line the horizon. The artist left the foreground and the peripheral areas blank. Though Whistler only completed one state of this lithograph, the stump work varies with the amount of ink applied during the printing, and the reflections in the canal water appear on early impressions that received the correct amount of ink. An incredible softness permeates this complex image; Whistler rendered the light and shadow with great subtlety. Using the stump, he conveyed deep shadows on the canal and lighter shadows on the buildings. Brightly illuminated gables thrust forward in contrast to the darker shadows around them. The image illustrates that Whistler employed a considerable range of tones, from the most delicate grays to small touches of harsh black. His lines never became mechanical, but remained vivacious throughout the image. JWR

1. Way and Dennis, *Memories of James McNeill Whistler*, p. 92.

2. Whistler to Thomas R. Way, September 20, 1893, Freer Gallery of Art, Smithsonian Institution, Washington, D.C. For the lithographs Whistler is specifically referring, see Chicago 62–65.

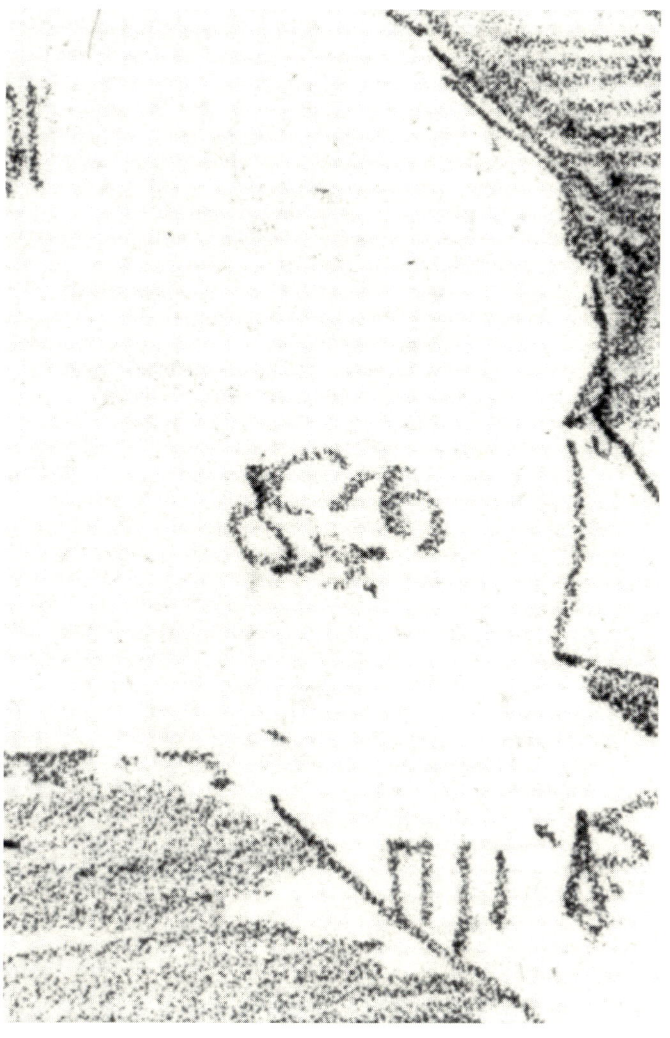

Detail from *Vitré, The Canal*, c. 1893
Lithograph on laid paper
Gift of Mr. and Mrs. Adolph Weil, Jr., in memory of Mr. and Mrs. Adolph Weil, Sr.
1992.2.18

Whistler both signed his prints individually, and at times used a design strategically placed within the composition to mark his works. This mark was a butterfly shape, which he both drew by hand to sign some works, and that he incorporated within others. In Vitré, *the butterfly floats above a rooftop on the right.*

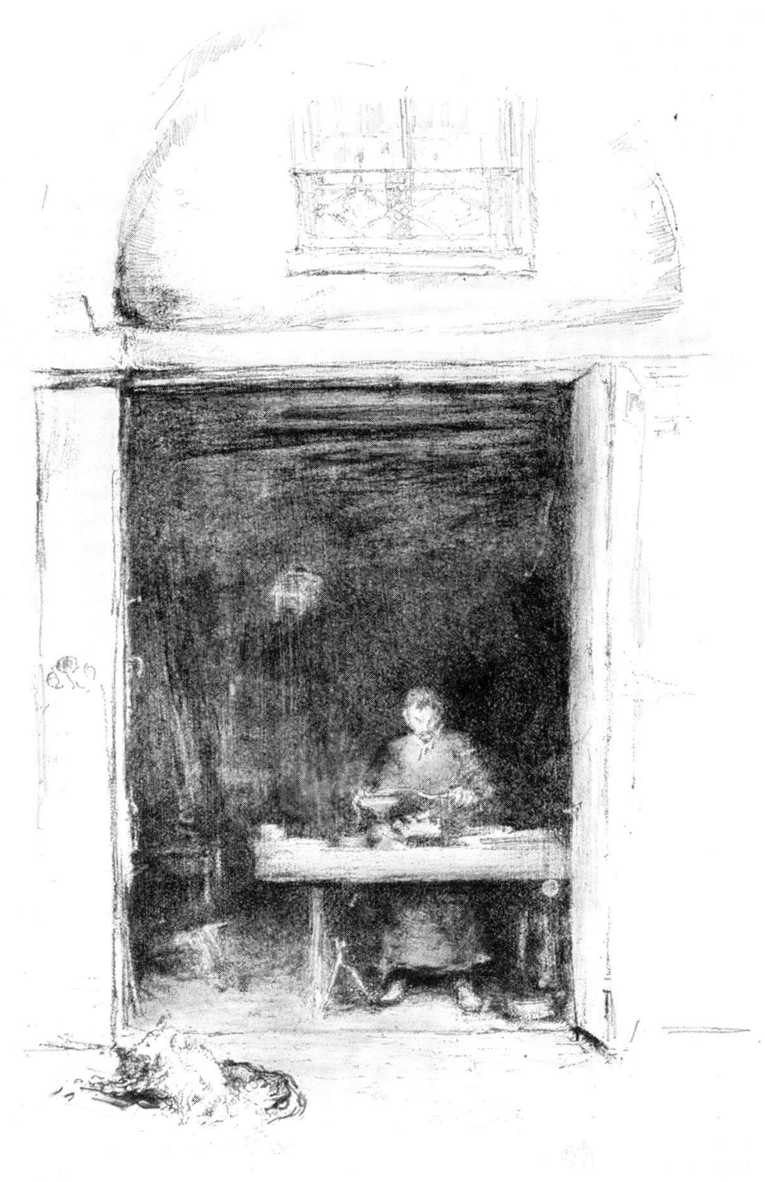

Lithograph
Wove paper
Signed, recto, center left in plate: artist's monogram (butterfly); lower right on sheet in graphite: artist's monogram (butterfly)
Chicago 103 ii/III; Way 73; Levy 109
Checklist 60

The Smith, Passage du Dragon, 1894

Printers Thomas Way and Thomas R. Way remained thoroughly involved throughout Whistler's engagement with transfer lithography. This arrangement allowed Whistler the freedom to approach his lithographs as simple sketches and removed him from the time-and labor-intensive processes of printing. In 1887, Messrs. Boussod, Valadon & Co. published the set of six lithographs known as Notes, thirty sets printed on large paper. After this printing run Whistler began to issue his lithographs separately, mostly as individual proofs on old Dutch paper. This limited the number of prints and allowed the artist and the printer to concentrate on one image at a time. Many were printed in small editions and were never published and rarely exhibited. Lithographs gave Whistler the opportunity to work with new effects, and they became almost personal, sacred works. And while the lithographs excited Whistler, they also allowed him to focus on other media.

Whistler sent *The Forge, Passage du Dragon* to Thomas R. Way for transferring and printing on August 22, 1894. He drew the sketch for it on smooth, thin, transparent paper commonly used in France as lithographic transfer paper. Papier Végétal, as it was known, is extremely fragile and shipping it to London for printing was complicated. During the next weeks Whistler continued to experiment with lithography, using new types of paper supplied by the French print firm Lemercier. This led to a second image of the site, this one titled *The Smith, Passage du Dragon* which he sent to Way on September 2. That paper proved even more fragile and did not hold up well to the rigors of travel. Whistler remained undaunted. He returned to the Passage du Dragon and worked on another specimen of paper from Lemercier's shop, which he described to Way as thin transfer paper mounted on a backing sheet. This method of attaching the transfer paper to a backing sheet had the added advantage of preventing the very thin paper from curling when laid on the stone. Way liked this new paper, but both it and unmounted papier végétal presented problems when he transferred the images to a stone. *The Smith*, in particular, resulted in an uneven distribution of ink throughout the image, so Whistler allowed the printers to rework the image by drawing directly onto the stone and eventually made adjustments himself when he traveled to London.

The Ways shared a unique artistic relationship with Whistler; the Way firm printed most of the 170 lithographic images that Whistler produced, and *The Smith, Passage du Dragon* reveals a lot about Whistler's creative artistic relationship with them. In this instance he allowed the Ways to make corrections to the image directly on the stone and accepted the printers' assistance and advice concerning the quality of the transfer paper. On September 14, 1894, Whistler wrote to Thomas Way and tried to analyze the problems they had faced with both images, beginning with *The Forge* and the unmounted papier végétal. The letter reveals also the measure of Whistler's respect for his colleague's opinion and guidance.

> Now let us distinguish—The two proofs are on two different papers. The failure is really I believe more my fault, than yours—Take the stump/fellow—My work here was not sharp enough and bright enough—It was too much nagged at—you like the paper—and I rather wore it out!

Then he addressed *The Smith*:

> The second little Forge was an old bit, and even it had some beautiful results—All the simple lines were of charming quality—shutters—top windows, etc—much prettier than in the other—and devoid of any of the grittiness of the usual "lithograph."[2]

Whistler retouched the stone of *The Smith, Passage du Dragon* about 1895, and made noteworthy changes. The prints from the first state were extremely faint. During the retouching Whistler extended the composition and darkened the lines that reinforced the shadows he had originally drawn. Although the earlier lithographs resemble simple chalk drawings, his later work with the stump produced remarkably different effects. As with *The Smith, Passage du Dragon,* Whistler experimented with multiple techniques to achieve a variety of textures. JWR

1. Whistler to Thomas R. Way, September 19, 1894, collection of Walter and Nesta Spink, Ann Arbor, Michigan. Folded sheet, written on all sides. Dated in pencil, in another hand, on first side: "19 Aug 1894."

2. Whistler to Thomas Way, September 14, 1894, Pennell-Whistler Collection, Manuscript Division, Library of Congress, Washington D.C.

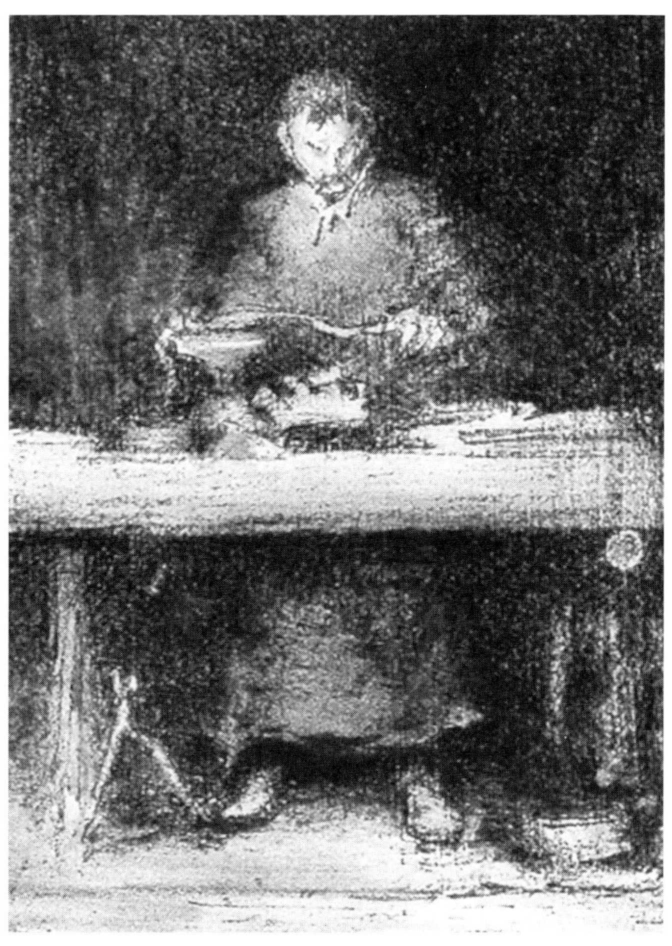

Detail from *The Smith, Passage du Dragon*, c. 1894
Lithograph on paper
Gift of Mr. and Mrs. Adolph Weil, Jr., in memory of Mr. and Mrs. Adolph Weil, Sr.
1992.2.18

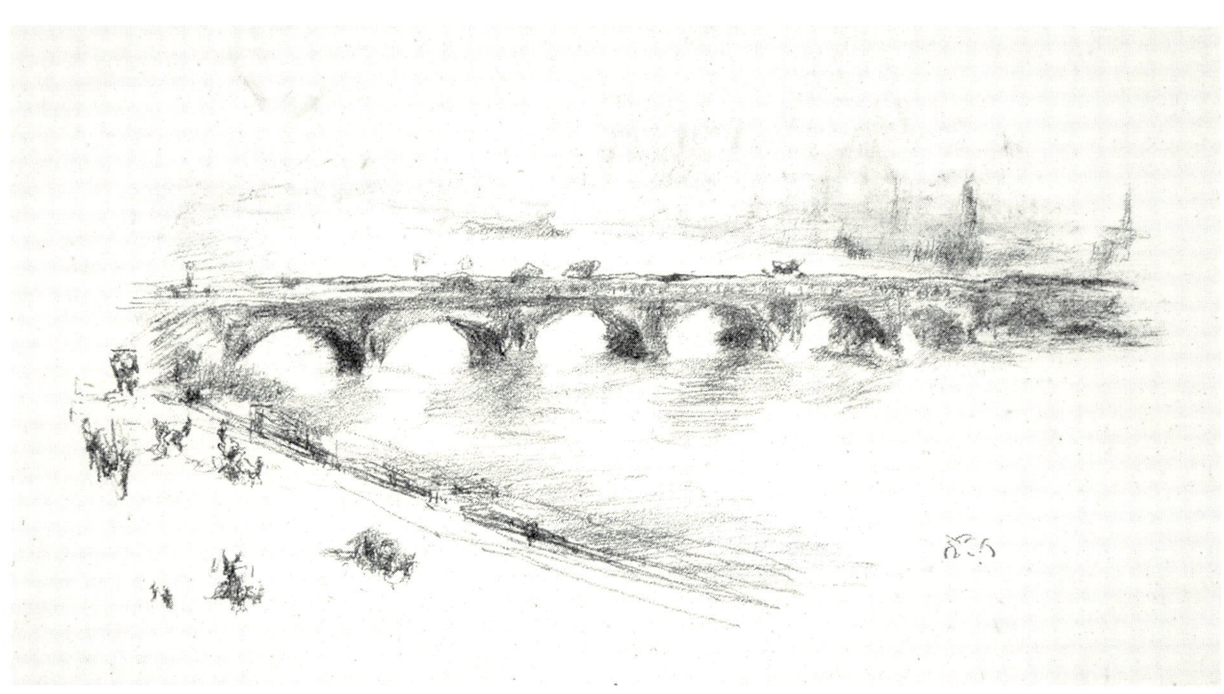

Lithograph
Japanese paper
Signed, recto, lower right in plate: artist's monogram (butterfly)
Chicago 155 ii/II; Way 119; Levy 165
Checklist 61

Evening, Little Waterloo Bridge, 1896

CATALOGUE ENTRY 28

The use of lithographic transfer paper allowed artists greater flexibility and ease in choosing where to work. Furthermore, unlike other traditional printmaking techniques such as woodcut, engraving, and etching, in which the impression is always a mirror image of the design on the block, or plate, or stone, in transfer lithography, the print is in the same direction as the original design, since the transfer process itself reverses the image twice, returning the image to its original orientation.

Whistler initially became interested in lithography in the late 1870s, but for a variety of reasons abandoned it until a decade later, remaining interested in the technique until 1896. His use of lithography partly is related to the circumstances of his personal and artistic life. In 1888, he married Beatrice Godwin, his beloved Trixie, and embarked upon what he would later recall as the happiest period of his life. During the early 1890s, Whistler enjoyed a level of personal, artistic, and financial success he had not experienced before. Devastatingly for Whistler, Beatrice was diagnosed with cancer in 1894.

Evening, Little Waterloo Bridge is one of eight lithographs Whistler drew from their rooms at the Savoy Hotel in London in February and March, 1896, where they stayed while Trixie was undergoing treatment. Lithography provided an important creative outlet for Whistler during this time. Trixie encouraged him, he was back in the vicinity of his printer Way, and transfer lithography allowed him to work and remain with his convalescent wife. *Evening, Little Waterloo Bridge* presents the view from Trixie's window looking east towards the bridge linking the Embankment with the same warehouses and wharves Whistler had etched many years earlier in the Thames Set.[1] The span of the bridge is the dominant feature of this composition, effectively dividing the two sides of the river. The Embankment, a popular riverside promenade space, sports just a few figures and vehicles. Long, darkening shadows, especially within the piers of the bridge and their reflections on the water, suggest the time of day. Although the artist drew the image on transfer paper, he subsequently added touches directly to the stone to enhance the atmospheric effects of the shadows and gathering mists.

The lithographs that Whistler made during Trixie's illness constitute some of his most personal ones; he created them primarily for dissemination among the family, only secondarily for a public offering. The MMFA impression belonged to Rosalind Birnie Philip, Beatrice's sister and the executor of Whistler's estate. Way only printed twenty-six images in 1896. Frederick Goulding printed a posthumous edition of forty-five impressions in 1904 before the stone was cancelled. EKJ

1. Stratis & Tedeschi, *Lithographs of James McNeill Whistler*, p. 442.

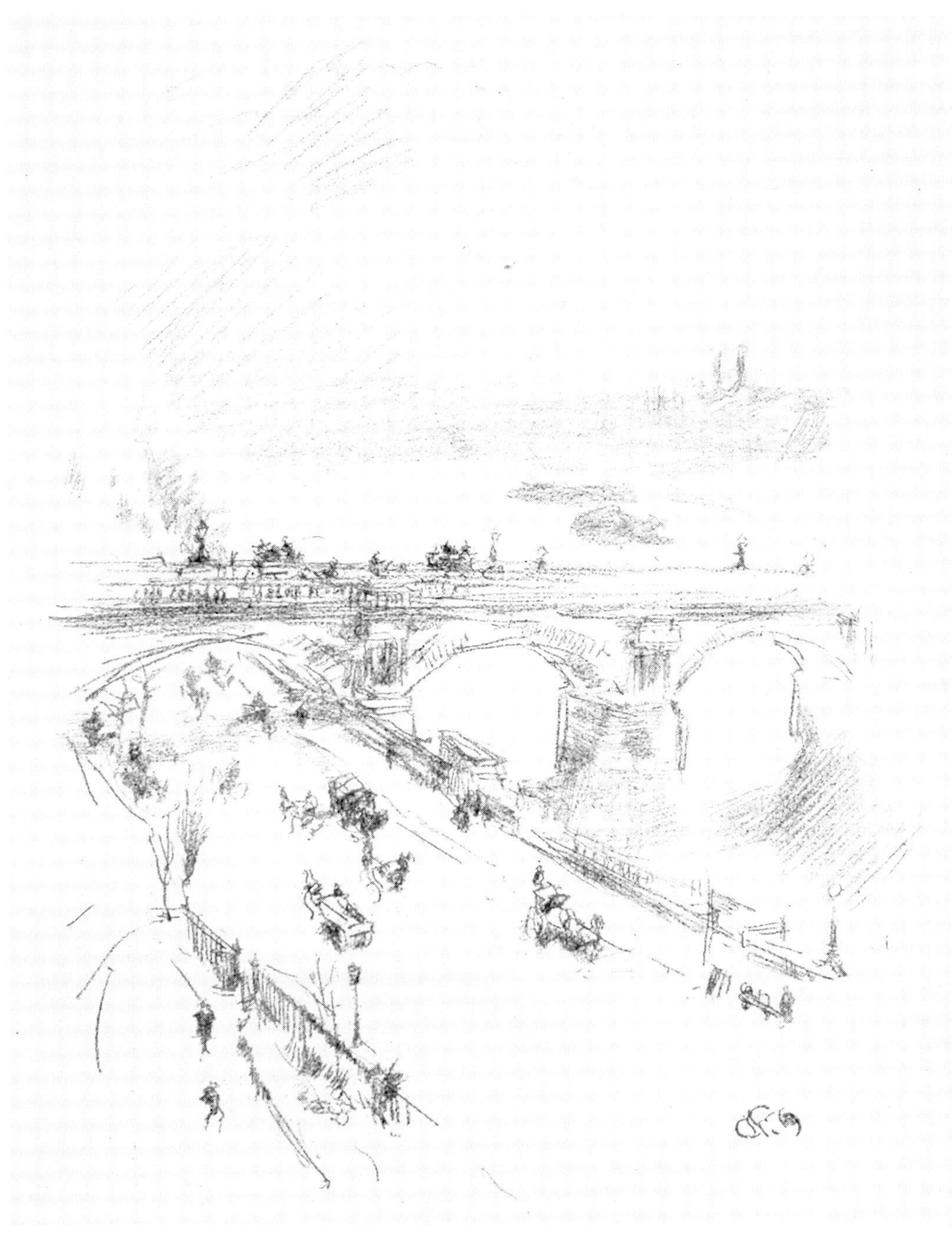

Lithograph
Laid paper
Signed, recto, lower right in plate: artist's monogram (butterfly)
Chicago 156 only state; Way 123;
Levy 177
Checklist 62

Waterloo Bridge, 1896

Trixie Whistler's illness prompted the couple to return to England at the end of 1894, and soon after the doctors diagnosed her disease as cancer. In February and March 1896, the Whistlers lived on the top floor of the Savoy in London. Their rooms offered a commanding vantage of the Thames at the great curve where the river shifts from a northerly direction to an easterly one. Of the eight lithographs Whistler produced during these months, six depicted the Thames from Trixie's window, and two offered intimate images of Trixie in her sickbed.[1]

Throughout his career Whistler found the great river a vital source of inspiration. He had published his first collection of images depicting the river, "Sixteen Etchings of Scenes on the Thames" (Thames Set), twenty-five years earlier. In 1896, he captured a different vision of life along the river with *Waterloo Bridge*.

The life and commerce of the River Thames defined nineteenth-century London. Inhabitants considered Waterloo Bridge an industrial achievement, a symbol of the new economic power of their city. Whistler's *Waterloo Bridge* represents a scene masked in the early morning mist looking east towards Blackfrairs Bridge. The bustle of city life appears as figures and carriages begin to emerge for the day. The lines of the print are very vivid and harsh. Whistler did not use the stump, and the bright areas within the print evoke the crisp morning air. The image can be understood as morning not only because of the bright areas he left clear, but because the artist also annotated an alternative title, *Waterloo Dawn*, on two proofs of the lithograph.

With *Waterloo Bridge* the artist strove to capture and provoke specific emotions. He deemphasized people and architecture and focused on the conditions of fog, rain or light on spatial areas of the print. There is a vivid contrast between the detailed treatment of the Embankment and the water, with the latter represented as a bright area absent of line. This makes it an important example of Whistler's more abstract late prints, which evoked a delicate aesthetic sense. As such *Waterloo Bridge* is both an ephemeral image of a subject that Whistler cherished and one of his most minimal compositions. Compared to etching, lithography had allowed the artist to manipulate a softer, more fluid line and texture that conveyed the delicacy of memory. *Waterloo Bridge* in particular is more suggestive than descriptive, and has links to the French symbolist movement. That movement was a collaboration of many different artists, and was manifested in many different forms, but was created in reaction to the realist and impressionist styles in art. Whistler maintained a close friendship and artistic collaboration with symbolist poet Stéphane Mallarmé, whom he met in 1886/87. The two shared a similar vision that emphasized personal expression in art. Mallarmé and Whistler supported and promoted each other's work. Mallarmé's poetry depicts an indispensable, universal reality that can only be understood by deconstructing layers of language and imagery. *Waterloo Bridge* must be read in the same manner, the details of the bridge and natural light in the landscape have the quality of actions remembered rather than experienced.

Waterloo Bridge, printed on March 19, 1896, became one of the last collaborations between Whistler and the Way printing firm. Whistler, in a great deal of distress concerning his wife's illness and subsequent death on May 10, 1896, quarreled with the printers over a catalogue of the artist's lithographs, and their relationship ended later that year. This break marked the end of Whistler's interest in lithography. JWR

1. *The Siesta* and *By the Balcony* (both at Freer Gallery of Art, Smithsonian Institution, Washington D.C.); see also Chicago 159, 160.

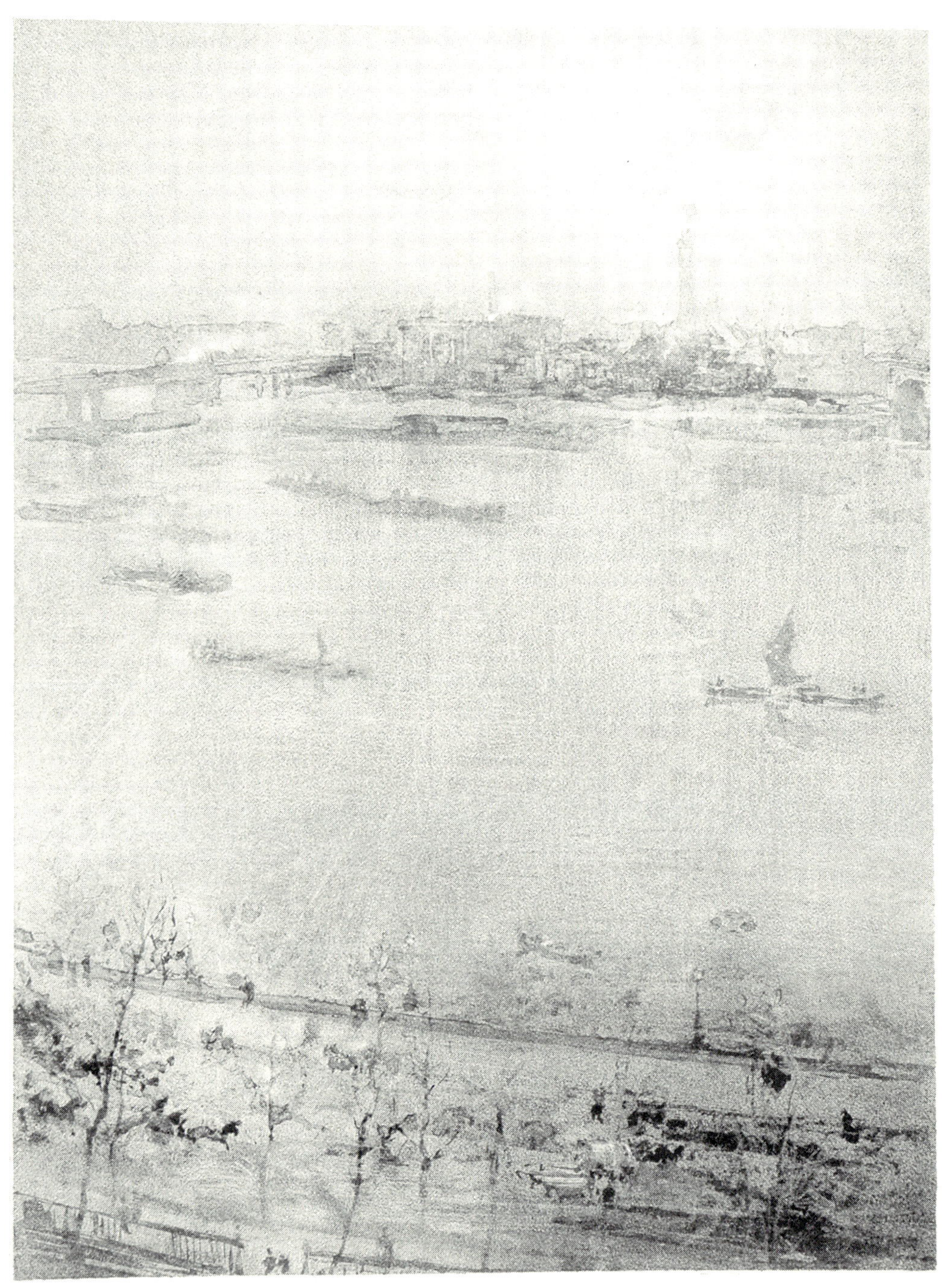

Lithotint
Wove proofing paper
Chicago 161 2/3; Way 125; Levy 179
Signed, recto, lower right on plate: artist's monogram (butterfly)
Checklist 63

The Thames, 1896

CATALOGUE ENTRY 30

Whistler's lithotint *The Thames*, one of the last and finest of the artist's printed nocturnes, was also the final one of the eight works done from the window of the Savoy Hotel where he and his wife Beatrice resided during the last months of her life. For this one, unlike the other seven, Whistler returned to working directly on the stone, utilizing the technique that he had first tried and abandoned eighteen years before.

According to Thomas R. Way, Whistler's printer, it was not easy for the artist to obtain the effects that he sought on this stone:

> Then you come to the subject opposite the hotel, "The Thames," a large wash drawing, a great triumph in the end, but only after it had given him infinite trouble. It was nearly twenty years since he had last used lithotint, and all the early subjects done with it were much simpler than that he had started on, which was full of infinite detail on a very small scale. A stone was prepared with a half-tint for him to add to and scrape out from. Unfortunately it was found that this tint was not level when the proofs of the first state were taken, and he had the stone back to the hotel, and scraped away as much as he could of the irregularity, and generally advanced the whole drawing very greatly. But he was not yet satisfied, and again went through the process of retouching and scraping, and finally produced what must rank as one of the masterpieces of lithography.[1]

Whistler was a perfectionist throughout his life, and he painstakingly reworked the stone in the hotel room at the Savoy so that he would be able to capture the silvery light on the river at dusk. Only about a half dozen prints were pulled of the first state, followed by about ten in the second state, among them the MMFA's delicate impression.

Unlike the earlier lithographs of the same year, Whistler drew his scene directly on the stone so that the print is in reverse of the actual site. The scene was of the southern bank of the River Thames, including the Shot Tower, encompassing the stretch of Surrey that extended from the Waterloo Bridge on the extreme right to the Charing Cross Bridge on the left. Whistler depicted a train and the steam coming from its engine crossing the span to the left. In the foreground is the Embankment. The scene is moody and overcast with clouds, perhaps reflecting the artist's own emotional state. For the composition, the artist relied on a vertical nocturne format that first had appeared in his paintings in the Chelsea Nocturnes of circa 1870. Whistler adopted the composition from a print that he did in Venice in 1879–80, *Upright Venice* (ILLUS. P. 104). Way may have sensed the same affinity, when many years later he described the appearance of the Embankment in these lithographs: "And in all of these we have the embankment full of traffic and his beloved hansoms, the gondolas of London, now so rapidly disappearing."[2] ED

1. Way, *Memories of J. M Whistler*, p. 127
2. Way, *Memories of J. M. Whistler*, p. 128

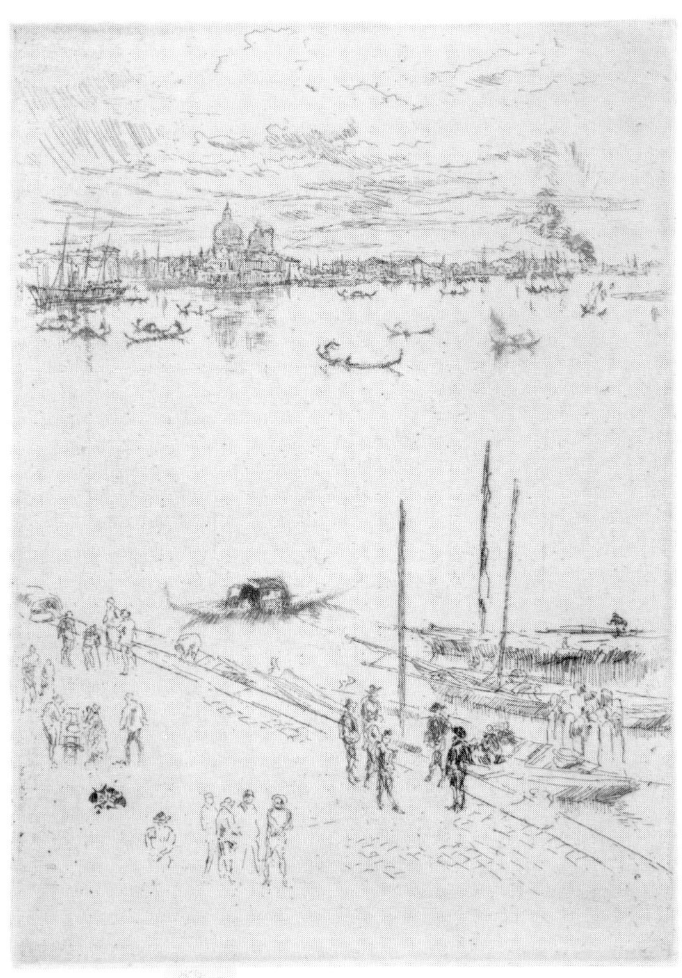

Upright Venice, 1879-80
Etching on paper
25.4 x 17.8 cm.
Freer Gallery of Art and Arthur M. Sackler Gallery, Washington D.C.
Gift of Charles Lang Freer
F1887.13

Checklist of the Exhibition

1. **Sketches on the Coast Survey Plate**
ca. 1854–55
Etching
Wove paper
Sheet: 7 7/8 x 11 1/8 in. (200 x 283 mm); image:
5 3/4 x 10 1/4 in. (146 x 260 mm)
Marks, verso, in graphite, center: "J.H. Wrenn Esq."; center right: "2032"; bottom center: "6 1/4 /10 5/8"; in ink, collector stamp, lower right: "J. H. W." in a rectangle (Lugt 1475)
Kennedy 1 only state; Mansfield 1
Provenance: John H. Wrenn, Chicago; Adolph Weil, Jr., Montgomery, Alabama
Montgomery Museum of Fine Arts, Gift of Mr. and Mrs. Adolph Weil, Jr., in memory of Mr. and Mrs. Adolph Weil, Sr.
1992.2.6

2. **Street at Saverne**
1858
One of "Twelve Etchings from Nature" (French Set)
Etching
Japanese paper
Sheet: 12 5/8 x 8 1/2 in. (321 x 216 mm); image: 8 1/4 x 6 1/4 in. (210 x 159 mm)
Signed, recto, lower left in plate: "Whistler"
Marks, recto, in graphite, lower right: "00748"
Kennedy 19 v/V; Mansfield 19
Provenance: Adolph Weil, Jr., Montgomery, Alabama
Montgomery Museum of Fine Arts, Gift of Mr. and Mrs. Adolph Weil, Jr., in memory of Mr. and Mrs. Adolph Weil, Sr.
1984.17.14

3. **La Vieille aux Loques**
1858
One of "Twelve Etchings from Nature" (French Set)
Etching
Laid paper
Sheet: 10 7/8 x 6 7/8 in. (276 x 175 mm); image: 8 1/4 x 5 7/8 in. (210 x 149 mm)
Signed, recto, lower right in plate: "Whistler"
Marks, recto, in graphite, bottom center: "12479" and "12333"; lower right: "N960"
Marks, verso, in graphite, lower left: "B1551/~~B144~~"; lower right: "CO"
Kennedy 21 iii/III; Mansfield 21
Provenance: Adolph Weil, Jr., Montgomery, Alabama
Montgomery Museum of Fine Arts, Gift of Mr. and Mrs. Adolph Weil, Jr., in memory of Mr. and Mrs. Adolph Weil, Sr.
1984.17.15

4. **The Kitchen**
1858
One of "Twelve Etchings from Nature" (French Set)
Etching
Wove paper
Sheet: 10 3/4 x 7 7/8 in. (273 x 200 mm); image: 8 15/16 x 6 3/16 in. (227 x 157 mm)
Signed, recto, lower right in plate: "Whistler"
Marks, recto, lower right in plate: "Imp. Delatrè. Rue St. Jac'ques. 171"
Kennedy 24 ii/III; Mansfield 24
Provenance: Adolph Weil, Jr., Montgomery, Alabama
Montgomery Museum of Fine Arts, Gift of Mr. and Mrs. Adolph Weil, Jr., in memory of Mr. and Mrs. Adolph Weil, Sr.
1992.2.7

5. Greenwich Park
1859
Etching
Laid paper
Sheet: 9 1/4 x 12 7/8 in. (235 x 327 mm); image: 5 x 8 in. (127 x 203 mm)
Signed, recto, lower left in plate: "Whistler"
Marks, recto, in graphite, upper right: "K 35II"; bottom center: "Greenwich Park 58556"; collector stamp in ink, lower left: "AB" in an oval (Lugt supp. 421)
Marks, verso, in graphite, center left: "No. 33 Greenwich Park/ 2eu Etat"; lower right corner: "55/72"
Kennedy 35 ii/II; Mansfield 34
Provenance: Alfred Beurdeley, Paris; Adolph Weil, Jr., Montgomery, Alabama
Montgomery Museum of Fine Arts, Gift of Mr. and Mrs. Adolph Weil, Jr., in memory of Mr. and Mrs. Adolph Weil, Sr.
1992.2.22

6. Greenwich Park
1859
Etching
Laid paper
Watermark: three circles with a cross above
Sheet: 8 x 12 1/2 in. (203 x 317 mm); image: 5 x 8 in. (127 x 203 mm)
Signed, recto, lower left in plate: "Whistler"
Marks, recto, in graphite, lower left: "Whistler K. 35 II Greenwich Park"; lower right: "C.23161"and "5"
Kennedy 35 ii/II; Mansfield 34
Provenance: Adolph Weil, Jr., Montgomery, Alabama
Montgomery Museum of Fine Arts, Gift of Mr. and Mrs. Adolph Weil, Jr., in memory of Mr. and Mrs. Adolph Weil, Sr.
1974.23

7. Thames Warehouses
1859
One of "Sixteen Etchings of Scenes of the Thames" (Thames Set)
Etching
Laid paper
Watermark: crowned griffin with a "P" and a dot below
Sheet: 4 5/8 x 10 in. (117 x 254 mm); image: 2 15/16 x 7 13/16 in. (75 x 198 mm)
Signed, recto, lower right in plate: "Whistler 1859"
Marks, recto, in graphite, lower left: "A66180 CHX" and "K.38 I-II/2"; lower right: "Thames Warehouses"
Marks, verso, in graphite, lower left: "35" in a circle; lower right: "£180"
Kennedy 38 ii/II; Mansfield 37
Provenance: Kennedy Galleries, New York; Adolph Weil, Jr., Montgomery, Alabama
Montgomery Museum of Fine Arts, Gift of Mr. and Mrs. Adolph Weil, Jr., in memory of Mr. and Mrs. Adolph Weil, Sr.
1984.17.1

8. Old Westminster Bridge
1859
Etching
Laid paper
Watermark: flourish design with DEQB above a brick-patterned shield
Sheet: 3 7/8 x 8 7/8 in. (98 x 225 mm); image: 3 x 7 15/16 in. (76 x 202 mm)
Signed, recto, lower left in plate: "Whistler 1859"
Kennedy 39 ii/II; Mansfield 38
Provenance: Adolph Weil, Jr., Montgomery, Alabama
Montgomery Museum of Fine Arts, Gift of Mr. and Mrs. Adolph Weil, Jr., in memory of Mr. and Mrs. Adolph Weil, Sr.
1984.17.2

9. Limehouse
1859
One of "Sixteen Etchings of Scenes of the Thames" (Thames Set)
Etching
Japanese paper (possibly gampi)
Sheet: 8 7/8 x 11 3/4 in. (225 x 298 mm); image: 5 x 8 in. (127 x 203 mm)
Signed, recto, lower right in plate: "Whistler 1859"
Marks, recto, in graphite, lower right: indecipherable
Kennedy 40 iii/III; Mansfield 39
Provenance: Adolph Weil, Jr., Montgomery, Alabama
Montgomery Museum of Fine Arts, Gift of Mr. and Mrs. Adolph Weil, Jr., in memory of Mr. and Mrs. Adolph Weil, Sr.
1984.17.3

10. Limehouse
1859
One of "Sixteen Etchings of Scenes of the Thames" (Thames Set)
Etching
Laid paper
Watermark: flourish design with DEQB above brick-patterned shield
Sheet: 5 7/8 x 9 in. (149 x 229 mm); image: 4 15/16 x 8 in. (125 x 203 mm)
Signed, recto, lower right in plate: "Whistler 1859"
Kennedy 40 iii/III; Mansfield 39
Provenance: Adolph Weil, Jr., Montgomery, Alabama
Montgomery Museum of Fine Arts, Gift of Mr. and Mrs. Adolph Weil, Jr., in memory of Mr. and Mrs. Adolph Weil, Sr.
1978.14

11. Eagle Wharf
1859
One of "Sixteen Etchings of Scenes of the Thames" (Thames Set)
Etching
Laid paper
Watermark: floral pattern
Sheet: 8 1/4 x 13 1/4 in. (210 x 337 mm); image: 5 7/16 x 8 7/16 in. (138 x 214 mm)
Signed, recto, bottom center in plate: "Whistler 1859"
Marks, recto, in graphite, lower left corner: "A16930"
Marks, verso, in graphite, lower left corner: "A79352"
Kennedy 41 only state; Mansfield 40
Provenance: Kennedy Galleries, New York; Adolph Weil, Jr., Montgomery, Alabama
Montgomery Museum of Fine Arts, Gift of Mr. and Mrs. Adolph Weil, Jr., in memory of Mr. and Mrs. Adolph Weil, Sr.
1984.17.4

12. Black Lion Wharf
1859
One of "Sixteen Etchings of Scenes of the Thames" (Thames Set)
Etching
Wove paper
Sheet: 7 7/16 x 10 1/2 in. (189 x 267 mm); image: 5 7/8 x 8 15/16 in. (149 x 227 mm)
Signed, recto, lower right in plate: "Whistler 1859"
Marks, verso, in graphite, lower left: "a7894" and "8267"; center right: "7894" and "~~7895~~"
Kennedy 42 iii/III; Mansfield 41
Provenance: Kennedy Galleries, New York; Adolph Weil, Jr., Montgomery, Alabama
Montgomery Museum of Fine Arts, Gift of Mr. and Mrs. Adolph Weil, Jr., in memory of Mr. and Mrs. Adolph Weil, Sr.
1984.17.5

13. The Pool
1859
One of "Sixteen Etchings of Scenes of the Thames" (Thames Set)
Etching
Laid paper
Watermark: crowned griffin
Sheet: 7 1/2 x 10 3/8 in. (191 x 264 mm); image: 5 1/2 x 8 1/2 in. (140 x 216 mm)
Signed, recto, lower left in plate: "Whistler 1859"
Marks, recto, in graphite, lower left: "AAA#6"; lower right: "D7504"
Kennedy 43 iv/IV; Mansfield 42
Provenance: Adolph Weil, Jr., Montgomery, Alabama
Montgomery Museum of Fine Arts, Gift of Mr. and Mrs. Adolph Weil, Jr., in memory of Mr. and Mrs. Adolph Weil, Sr.
1984.17.6

14. Thames Police (Wapping Wharf)
1859
One of "Sixteen Etchings of Scenes of the Thames" (Thames Set)
Etching
Japanese paper
Sheet: 7 3/16 x 10 1/16 in. (183 x 256 mm); image: 6 x 9 in. (152 x 229 mm)
Signed, recto, lower right in plate: "Whistler 1859"
Marks, recto, in graphite, bottom center: "7802"
Marks, verso, in graphite, lower left: "AAA-7"
Kennedy 44 iii/III; Mansfield 43
Provenance: Adolph Weil, Jr., Montgomery, Alabama
Montgomery Museum of Fine Arts, Gift of Mr. and Mrs. Adolph Weil, Jr., in memory of Mr. and Mrs. Adolph Weil, Sr.
1984.17.7

15. Longshoremen
1859
Etching
Laid paper
Sheet: 7 1/8 x 10 in. (181 x 254 mm); image: 6 x 8 15/16 in. (152 x 227 mm)
Signed, recto, lower right in plate: "Whistler 1859"; lower left on sheet, in graphite: artist's monogram (butterfly)
Marks, verso, in graphite, lower left: "A20460"
Kennedy 45 only state; Mansfield 44
Provenance: Kennedy Galleries, New York; Adolph Weil, Jr., Montgomery, Alabama
Montgomery Museum of Fine Arts, Gift of Mr. and Mrs. Adolph Weil, Jr., in memory of Mr. and Mrs. Adolph Weil, Sr.
1992.2.8

16. The Lime-Burner
1859
One of "Sixteen Etchings of Scenes of the Thames" (Thames Set)
Etching
Laid paper
Watermark: KF
Sheet: 14 1/2 x 9 3/16 in. (368 x 233 mm); image: 9 7/8 x 6 15/16 in. (251 x 176 mm)
Signed, recto, lower right in plate: "Whistler 1859"
Marks, recto, in graphite, lower left: "a59317"
Kennedy 46 ii/II; Mansfield 45
Provenance: Kennedy Galleries, New York; Adolph Weil, Jr., Montgomery, Alabama
Montgomery Museum of Fine Arts, Gift of Mr. and Mrs. Adolph Weil, Jr., in memory of Mr. and Mrs. Adolph Weil, Sr.
1984.17.8

17. Billingsgate

1859

Etching and drypoint

Japanese paper

Sheet: 7 1/2 x 10 1/8 in. (191 x 257 mm); image: 6 1/16 x 9 in. (154 x 229 mm)

Signed, recto, lower right in plate: "Whistler 1859"

Marks, recto, in graphite, bottom center: "47iv"

Marks, verso, in graphite, lower left: "B7467"; lower right: "YH"

Kennedy 47 viii/VIII; Mansfield 46

Provenance: William Weston Gallery, London; Adolph Weil, Jr., Montgomery, Alabama

Montgomery Museum of Fine Arts, Gift of Mr. and Mrs. Adolph Weil, Jr., in memory of Mr. and Mrs. Adolph Weil, Sr.

1992.2.9

18. Soupe à Trois Sous

1859

Drypoint

Japanese paper

Sheet: 8 1/8 x 12 1/8 in. (206 x 308 mm); image: 6 x 9 in. (152 x 229 mm)

Signed, recto, upper center in plate: "Whistler"

Marks, recto, in graphite, lower right: "ax 945"

Marks, verso, in graphite, lower left: "A 93049"; lower right: "EH"

Kennedy 49 only state; Mansfield 49

Provenance: Kennedy Galleries, New York; Adolph Weil, Jr., Montgomery, Alabama

Montgomery Museum of Fine Arts, Gift of Mr. and Mrs. Adolph Weil, Jr., in memory of Mr. and Mrs. Adolph Weil, Sr.

1992.2.23

19. Becquet

1859

One of "Sixteen Etchings of Scenes of the Thames" (Thames Set)

Drypoint

Laid paper

Watermark: coat of arms below a crown and cross

Sheet: 14 1/8 x 9 1/8 in. (359 x 232 mm); image: 10 x 7 1/2 in. (254 x 191 mm)

Marks, recto, upper right, in graphite: "K52 III/IV"; lower left, in graphite: "R1887N"; collector stamp in ink: "AB" in oval (Lugt 421)

Marks, verso, in graphite, lower left: "The Fiddler"; lower right: "68/7e"

Kennedy 52 iii/IV; Mansfield 52

Provenance: Alfred Beurdeley, Paris; William H. Schab Gallery, New York

Montgomery Museum of Fine Arts, Gift of Mr. and Mrs. Adolph Weil, Jr., in memory of Mr. and Mrs. Adolph Weil, Sr.

1986.3

20. Drouet

1859

Drypoint

Laid paper

Watermark: outline of a castle

Sheet: 11 1/2 x 8 1/16 in. (292 x 205 mm); image: 9 1/16 x 6 in. (230 x 152 mm)

Signed, recto, lower right in plate: "Whistler 1859"

Marks, recto, in plate, bottom center: "Drouet Sculpteur"; upper right: "Whistler Inouie Eaux Fortes"

Marks, verso, in graphite, lower left: "A79272"

Kennedy 55 ii/II; Mansfield 55

Provenance: Kennedy Galleries, New York; William H. Schab Gallery, New York, 1986

Montgomery Museum of Fine Arts, Gift of Mr. and Mrs. Adolph Weil, Jr., in memory of Mr. and Mrs. Adolph Weil, Sr.

1986.8

21. Rotherhithe

1860

One of "Sixteen Etchings of Scenes of the Thames" (Thames Set)

Etching

Laid paper

Sheet: 14 3/8 x 9 1/8 in. (365 x 232 mm); image: 10 3/4 x 7 3/4 in. (273 x 197 mm)

Signed, recto, lower left in plate: "Whistler 1860"

Marks, verso, in graphite, lower left: "A43628"

Kennedy 66 iii/III; Mansfield 66

Provenance: Kennedy Galleries, New York; Adolph Weil, Jr., Montgomery, Alabama.

Montgomery Museum of Fine Arts, Gift of Mr. and Mrs. Adolph Weil, Jr., in memory of Mr. and Mrs. Adolph Weil, Sr.

1984.17.9

22. The Forge

1861

One of "Sixteen Etchings of Scenes of the Thames" (Thames Set)

Etching

Japanese paper

Sheet: 8 7/8 x 13 1/2 in. (225 x 343 mm); image: 7 3/4 x 12 1/2 in. (197 x 318 mm)

Signed, recto, lower right in plate: "Whistler 1861"

Marks, recto, in graphite, lower right: "C181, K. 68a"; bottom center: "2£f" or "Z£f"

Kennedy 68 iii/IV; Mansfield 68

Provenance: Adolph Weil, Jr., Montgomery, Alabama

Montgomery Museum of Fine Arts, Gift of Mr. and Mrs. Adolph Weil, Jr., in memory of Mr. and Mrs. Adolph Weil, Sr.

1984.17.10

23. Vauxhall Bridge
1861
Etching
Laid paper
Sheet: 4 x 5 3/4 in. (102 x 146 mm); image: 2 3/4 x 4 1/2 in. (70 x 114 mm)
Signed, recto, lower right in plate: "Whistler 1861"
Marks, recto, in graphite, lower right corner: "K674"
Kennedy 70 ii/II; Mansfield 70
Provenance: Adolph Weil, Jr., Montgomery, Alabama
Montgomery Museum of Fine Arts, Gift of Mr. and Mrs. Adolph Weil, Jr., in memory of Mr. and Mrs. Adolph Weil, Sr.
1984.17.13

24. Millbank
1861
One of "Sixteen Etchings of Scenes of the Thames" (Thames Set)
Etching
Japanese paper (possibly gampi)
Sheet: 6 x 7 3/8 in. (152 x 187 mm); image: 4 x 5 in. (102 x 127 mm)
Marks, recto, lower left in plate: "1861"; on sheet, in graphite, lower right: "S.2586"; lower left: "W67 & K71" and "Millbank K44 III"
Kennedy 71 v/V; Mansfield 71
Provenance: Adolph Weil, Jr., Montgomery, Alabama
Montgomery Museum of Fine Arts, Gift of Mr. and Mrs. Adolph Weil, Jr., in memory of Mr. and Mrs. Adolph Weil, Sr.
1984.17.11

25. The Little Pool
1861
One of "Sixteen Etchings of Scenes of the Thames" (Thames Set)
Etching
Wove paper
Sheet: 8 7/16 x 9 7/8 in. (214 x 251 mm); 4 x 4 7/8 in. (102 x 124 mm)
Signed, recto, center left in plate: "Whistler 1861"
Marks, verso, in graphite, center left: "77298"; center right: "J[?]W."
Kennedy 74 v/VIII; Mansfield 73
Provenance: Robert Dance, Inc., New York, 1985
Montgomery Museum of Fine Arts, Gift of Mr. and Mrs. Adolph Weil, Jr., in memory of Mr. and Mrs. Adolph Weil, Sr.
1985.9

26. Early Morning, Battersea
1861
One of "Sixteen Etchings of Scenes of the Thames" (Thames Set)
Etching
Japanese paper (possibly gampi)
Sheet: 6 5/16 x 9 3/8 in. (160 x 238 mm); image: 4 1/2 x 6 in. (114 x 152 mm)
Signed, recto, lower left in plate: "Whistler"
Marks, recto, in graphite, lower right: "P826.6"; upper left corner: "46 4/4"
Kennedy 75 only state; Mansfield 75
Provenance: Childs Gallery, Boston, 1985
Montgomery Museum of Fine Arts, Gift of Mr. and Mrs. Adolph Weil, Jr., in memory of Mr. and Mrs. Adolph Weil, Sr.
1985.13

27. Old Hungerford Bridge
1861
One of "Sixteen Etchings of Scenes of the Thames" (Thames Set)
Etching
Japanese paper (possibly gampi)
Sheet: 7 5/16 x 9 7/8 in. (186 x 251 mm); image: 5 7/16 x 8 3/8 in. (138 x 213 mm)
Signed, recto, lower right in plate: "Whistler"
Marks, recto, in graphite, lower right: "7753"
Kennedy 76 iii/III; Mansfield 76
Provenance: Robert Dance, Inc., New York, 1985
Montgomery Museum of Fine Arts, Gift of Mr. and Mrs. Adolph Weil, Jr. in memory of Mr. and Mrs. Adolph Weil, Sr.
1985.2

28. Amsterdam, from the Tolhuis
1863
Etching and drypoint
Laid paper
Sheet: 8 3/16 x 11 1/2 in. (208 x 292 mm); image: 5 1/4 x 8 1/4 in. (133 x 210 mm)
Signed, recto, lower right in plate: "Whistler 1863" and artist's monogram (butterfly); on sheet, lower right, in graphite: artist's monogram (butterfly) and "imp."
Marks, recto, lower right in plate: "a Amsterdam Tolhuis"
Marks, verso, in graphite, bottom center: "02137"; lower right: "U91" and "EXV"; lower left, collector stamp in ink: "TD" in an oval (Lugt 2427)
Kennedy 91 iv/IV; Mansfield 91
Provenance: Tracy Dows, New York; Christie's New York, sale 5213, November 5, 1982, lot no. 107; Adolph Weil, Jr., Montgomery, Alabama
Montgomery Museum of Fine Arts, Gift of Jean K. Weil in memory of Adolph "Bucks" Weil, Jr.
1999.7.133

29. Chelsea Bridge and Church
1870–71
One of "Sixteen Etchings of Scenes of the Thames" (Thames Set)
Etching
Laid paper
Sheet: 6 1/2 x 9 1/4 in. (165 x 235 mm); image: 4 x 6 5/8 in. (102 x 168 mm)
Marks, recto, in graphite, lower left: "CHELSEA BRIDGE + CHURCH K95 III"
Kennedy 95 vi/VI; Mansfield 96
Provenance: Adolph Weil, Jr., Montgomery, Alabama
Montgomery Museum of Fine Arts, Gift of Mr. and Mrs. Adolph Weil, Jr., in memory of Mr. and Mrs. Adolph Weil, Sr.
1984.17.12

30. Battersea: Dawn
1875
Drypoint
Laid paper
Watermark: arms of Amsterdam (Chicago 8)
Sheet: 8 5/16 x 13 3/8 in. (211 x 340 mm); image: 5 7/8 x 8 7/8 in. (149 x 225 mm)
Signed, recto, upper right in plate: artist's monogram (butterfly)
Marks, recto, in graphite, lower left: "Battersea Dawn 1st St"; bottom center, in graphite: "Battersea"
Marks, verso, in graphite, lower left: "JE P-2"; bottom center: "73362"; collector stamps in ink, lower right: ornate "D" (Lugt 716) and "M" superimposed over "H" in a circle (Lugt 1342); center: "HW" (Lugt 2532)
Kennedy 155 i/IV; Mansfield 152
Provenance: Theodore Agnew & Sons, London, 1906; Bibliotheque Royal de Windsor, London; Howard Mansfield, New York; Judson S. Dutcher, Ellenville, New York; Adolph Weil, Jr., Montgomery, Alabama
Montgomery Museum of Fine Arts, Gift of Mr. and Mrs. Adolph Weil, Jr., in memory of Mr. and Mrs. Adolph Weil, Sr.
1992.2.10

31. St. James's Street
1878
Etching and drypoint
Laid paper
Watermark: shield with HP in the center, surrounded by crossed branches
Sheet: 13 3/4 x 8 1/4 in. (349 x 210 mm); image: 10 15/16 x 5 15/16 in. (278 x 151 mm)
Signed, recto, lower left in plate: artist's monogram (butterfly)
Marks, recto, in graphite, bottom center: "K169 IV/4"; lower right: "C.3746O[?]
Kennedy 169 iv/IV; Mansfield 165
Provenance: P. & D. Colnaghi & Co., London, 1970
Montgomery Museum of Fine Arts, Gift of Mrs. Julian Wiener, Mrs. Stanley Newhouse, and James Loeb in honor of their father, Lucien S. Loeb
1970.14

32. The "Adam and Eve," Old Chelsea
1879
Etching
Laid paper
Sheet: 10 3/4 x 17 7/8 in. (273 x 454 mm); image: 6 15/16 x 12 in. (176 x 305 mm)
Signed, recto, upper left in plate: artist's monogram (butterfly)
Marks, verso, in graphite, lower left: "A73226A"
Kennedy 175 ii/II; Mansfield 172
Provenance: Kennedy Galleries, New York; Adolph Weil, Jr., Montgomery, Alabama
Montgomery Museum of Fine Arts, Gift of Mr. and Mrs. Adolph Weil, Jr., in memory of Mr. and Mrs. Adolph Weil, Sr.
1984.17.17

33. Little Venice
1879–80
One of "Twelve Etchings" (First Venice Set)
Etching
Laid paper
Watermark: VG (possibly a Van Gelder countermark)
Sheet, trimmed to plate: 7 1/4 x 10 1/2 in. (184 x 267 mm)
Signed, recto, lower left in plate: artist's monogram (butterfly); lower left on tab, in graphite: artist's monogram (butterfly) and "imp."; verso, in graphite, lower right: artist's monogram (butterfly) and "imp"
Marks, verso, in graphite, lower left: "iS–"; "MK [or NK] • 38531"; "a25251"; collector stamp in ink, in center: twice, both illegible
Kennedy 183 only state; Mansfield 180
Provenance: Kennedy Galleries, New York; Sotheby's, New York, sale of May 11, 1989; Adolph Weil, Jr., Montgomery, Alabama
Montgomery Museum of Fine Arts, Gift of Jean K. Weil in memory of Adolph "Bucks" Weil, Jr.
1999.7.134

34. Nocturne
1879–80
One of "Twelve Etchings" (First Venice Set)
Etching and drypoint
Laid paper
Watermark: arms of Amsterdam with IV countermark (Chicago 194)
Sheet, trimmed to plate: 8 x 11 11/16 in. (203 x 297 mm)
Signed, recto, in graphite, lower left on tab,: artist's monogram (butterfly) and "imp."
Marks, verso, in graphite, lower left: "a 15358"; lower right: "nm"
Kennedy 184 iv/V; Mansfield 181
Provenance: Sotheby's, New York, sale of May 3, 1984; Kennedy Galleries, New York; Adolph Weil, Jr., Montgomery, Alabama
Montgomery Museum of Fine Arts, Gift of Jean K. Weil in memory of Adolph "Bucks" Weil, Jr.
1999.7.135

35. The Little Mast

1879–80

One of "Twelve Etchings" (First Venice Set)

Etching and drypoint

Laid paper

Sheet: 12 1/8 x 8 1/2 in. (308 x 216 mm); image: 10 1/2 x 7 3/8 in. (310 x 216 mm)

Signed, recto, upper right in plate: artist's monogram (butterfly); on sheet, in graphite, lower left: artist's monogram (butterfly) and "imp."

Marks, recto, in graphite, bottom center: "#30529"

Marks, verso, in graphite, lower left: "The Little Mast K 185"; collector stamp in ink, lower left: a crown above "V" and "R" in an oval (Lugt 2535)

Kennedy 185 iii/IV; Mansfield 182

Provenance: Bibliotheque Royale de Windsor, London; Sotheby's, New York, sale of May 6, 1981; Adolph Weil, Jr., Montgomery, Alabama

Montgomery Museum of Fine Arts, Gift of Jean K. Weil in memory of Adolph "Bucks" Weil, Jr.

1999.7.136

36. The Doorway

1879–80

One of "Twelve Etchings" (First Venice Set)

Etching and drypoint

Laid paper

Sheet, trimmed to plate: 11 1/2 x 7 15/16 in. (292 x 202 mm)

Signed, recto, upper left in plate: artist's monogram (butterfly); in graphite, lower left on tab: artist's monogram (butterfly) and "imp."

Marks, verso, in graphite, lower left: "K4346/ ~~a 60573~~

a 64272"; center: "68552 W.154"; lower right: "K.188-6 sur 7"

Kennedy 188 vi/VII; Mansfield 185

Provenance: Kennedy Galleries; Sotheby's, New York, sale of November 21, 1981; Adolph Weil, Jr., Montgomery, Alabama

Montgomery Museum of Fine Arts, Gift of Jean K. Weil in memory of Adolph "Bucks" Weil, Jr.

1999.7.137

37. The Piazzetta

1879–80

One of "Twelve Etchings" (First Venice Set)

Etching

Japanese paper

Sheet, trimmed to plate: 10 x 7 in. (254 x 178 mm)

Signed, recto, lower left in plate: artist's monogram (butterfly); in graphite, lower left on tab: artist's monogram (butterfly) and "imp."

Marks, verso, in graphite, lower left: "PIAZETTA K 189"

Kennedy 189 iii/V; Mansfield 186

Provenance: Sotheby's, New York, sale of May 29, 1980; Adolph Weil, Jr., Montgomery, Alabama.

Montgomery Museum of Fine Arts, Gift of Jean K. Weil in memory of Adolph "Bucks" Weil, Jr.

1999.7.138

38. The Traghetto, No. 2

1879–80

One of "Twelve Etchings" (First Venice Set)

Etching and drypoint

Laid paper

Sheet, trimmed to plate: 9 1/2 x 12 1/16 in. (241 x 306 mm)

Signed, recto, left center in plate: artist's monogram (butterfly); verso, in graphite, lower left,: artist's monogram (butterfly) and "imp."

Marks, verso, in graphite, lower left: "a 32136"; bottom center: "The Traghetto / very early proof / W.156"; lower right: "959a" or "959o"; "17/17"; "134"

Kennedy 191 iii/IV; Mansfield 188

Provenance: Kennedy Galleries, New York; Sotheby's, New York, sale of November 18–19, 1982; Adolph Weil, Jr., Montgomery, Alabama

Montgomery Museum of Fine Arts, Gift of Jean K. Weil in memory of Adolph "Bucks" Weil, Jr.

1999.7.139

39. The Riva, No. 1

1879–80

One of "Twelve Etchings" (First Venice Set)

Etching

Laid paper

Watermark: "Fellows" (Chicago 119)

Sheet, trimmed to plate: 7 13/16 x 11 5/8 in. (203 x 295 mm)

Signed, recto, upper left in plate: artist's monogram (butterfly); lower left on tab, in graphite: artist's monogram (butterfly) and "imp."

Marks, verso, in graphite, lower left: "A 16304"; center: "02138"; bottom center: "The Riva"; lower right: "K192"

Kennedy 192 iii/III; Mansfield 189

Provenance: Kennedy Galleries, New York, August 27, 1970; Adolph Weil, Jr., Montgomery, Alabama

Montgomery Museum of Fine Arts, Gift of Jean K. Weil in memory of Adolph "Bucks" Weil, Jr.

1999.7.140

40. Two Doorways

1879–80

One of "Twelve Etchings" (First Venice Set)

Etching and drypoint

Laid paper

Watermark: "1814/2" (Chicago 325)

Sheet, trimmed to plate: 8 1/8 x 11 9/16 in. (206 x 294 mm)

Signed, recto, upper left in plate: artist's monogram (butterfly); in graphite, lower left on tab: artist's monogram (butterfly) and "imp."

Kennedy 193 iv/VI; Mansfield 190

Provenance: William Schab Gallery, 1984; Adolph Weil, Jr., Montgomery, Alabama

Montgomery Museum of Fine Arts, Gift of Jean K. Weil in memory of Adolph "Bucks" Weil, Jr.

1999.7.141

41. The Beggars

1879–80

One of "Twelve Etchings" (First Venice Set)

Etching and drypoint

Japanese paper

Sheet: 12 5/8 x 9 in. (321 x 229 mm); image: 12 x 8 1/4 in. (305 x 210 mm)

Signed, recto, in graphite, lower left: artist's monogram (butterfly) and "imp."

Marks, verso, in graphite, lower left: "a30847"; collector stamp in ink, lower left: "J.H.W." in a rectangle (Lugt 1475)

Kennedy 194 ix/IX: Mansfield 191

Provenance: John H. Wrenn, Chicago; Kennedy Galleries, New York; Adolph Weil, Jr., Montgomery, Alabama

Montgomery Museum of Fine Arts, Gift of Mr. and Mrs. Adolph Weil, Jr., in memory of Mr. and Mrs. Adolph Weil, Sr.

1992.2.11

42. The Mast

1879–80

One of "Twelve Etchings" (First Venice Set)

Etching

Laid paper

Watermark: Strasbourg lily (Chicago 284)

Sheet, trimmed to plate: 13 1/2 x 6 7/16 in. (343 x 164 mm); with added margins: 16 1/2 x 9 7/16 in. (419 x 240 mm)

Signed, recto, center left in plate: artist's monogram (butterfly); in graphite, lower left on tab: artist's monogram (butterfly) and "imp."; verso, in graphite, lower right: artist's monogram (butterfly)

Marks, verso, in graphite, bottom center: "The Mast, Venice./ with Whistler's autograph and monogram-/ "chosen proof"; lower right, in the artist's hand: chosen proof.

Kennedy 195 v/VI; Mansfield 192

Provenance: Adolph Weil, Jr., Montgomery, Alabama

Montgomery Museum of Fine Arts, Gift of Mr. and Mrs. Adolph Weil, Jr., in memory of Mr. and Mrs. Adolph Weil, Sr.

1992.2.12

43. San Biagio

1879–80

One of "Twenty-Six Etchings" (Second Venice Set)

Etching and drypoint

Laid paper

Watermark: Strasbourg lily / WR (Chicago 300)

Sheet, trimmed to plate: 8 3/8 x 12 1/16 in. (213 x 306 mm)

Signed, recto, center left in plate: artist's monogram (butterfly); lower left on tab, in graphite: artist's monogram (butterfly) and "imp."

Marks, verso, lower left, in graphite: "a39295"; upper right: "8/8/•"; collector stamp in ink, lower right: initials "HHB" (Lugt 2936)

Kennedy 197 ii/IX; Mansfield 194; proof state, not from published set

Provenance: Henry Harper Benedict, New York; Kennedy Galleries, New York; Adolph Weil, Jr., Montgomery, Alabama

Montgomery Museum of Fine Arts, Gift of Jean K. Weil in memory of Adolph "Bucks" Weil, Jr.

1999.7.142

44. Nocturne: Palaces

1879–80

One of "Twenty-Six Etchings" (Second Venice Set)

Etching and drypoint

Laid paper

Watermark: Strasbourg lily / WR (Chicago 300)

Sheet, trimmed to plate: 11 3/4 x 8 in. (299 x 203 mm)

Signed, recto, in graphite, lower left on tab: artist's monogram (butterfly) and "imp."

Kennedy 202 vii/IX; Mansfield 199

Provenance: William Schab Gallery, New York 1986; Adolph Weil, Jr., Montgomery, Alabama

Montgomery Museum of Fine Arts, Gift of Jean K. Weil in memory of Adolph "Bucks" Weil, Jr.

1999.7.143

45. Long Lagoon

1879–80

One of "Twenty-Six Etchings" (Second Venice Set)

Drypoint

Laid paper

Sheet, trimmed to plate: 6 1/4 x 9 1/16 in. (159 x 230 mm)

Signed, recto, in graphite, lower left on tab: artist's monogram (butterfly) and "imp. 2nd proof"

Marks, verso, in graphite, lower left: "169," "a 37042," and "122014.3 OMXX"; bottom center: "4389"; lower right: "Fox 2st Ø"

Kennedy 203 ii/II; Mansfield 200

Provenance: Kennedy Galleries, New York, May 2, 1980; Adolph Weil, Jr., Montgomery, Alabama

Montgomery Museum of Fine Arts, Gift of Jean K. Weil in memory of Adolph "Bucks" Weil, Jr.

1999.7.144

46. The Riva, No. 2

1879–80

One of "Twenty-Six Etchings" (Second Venice Set)

Etching

Laid paper

Kennedy 206 ii/II; Mansfield 203

Sheet, trimmed to plate: 8 1/4 x 12 1/16 in. (206 x 306 mm)

Signed, recto, upper left in plate: artist's monogram (butterfly); in graphite, lower left on tab: artist's monogram (butterfly) and "imp."

Marks, verso, in graphite, lower left: "P79"; lower right: "W234"; collector stamp in ink, center left: "TD" in an oval (Lugt 2427)

Provenance: Tracy Dows, New York; Sotheby Parke-Bernet, New York, sale of May 6, 1975; Adolph Weil, Jr., Montgomery, Alabama

Montgomery Museum of Fine Arts, Gift of Jean K. Weil in memory of Adolph "Bucks" Weil, Jr.

1999.7.145

47. The Balcony
1879–80
One of "Twenty-Six Etchings" (Second Venice Set)
Etching and drypoint
Laid paper
Watermark: coat of arms
Sheet, trimmed to plate: 11 11/16 x 7 7/8 in. (297 x 200 mm)
Signed, recto, upper left in plate: artist's monogram (butterfly); in graphite, lower left on tab: artist's monogram (butterfly) and "imp."
Marks, verso, in graphite, center: "13"; lower left: "H.P. 47"
Kennedy 207 iii/XI; Mansfield 204
Provenance: Adolph Weil, Jr., Montgomery, Alabama
Montgomery Museum of Fine Arts, Gift of Jean K. Weil in memory of Adolph "Bucks" Weil, Jr.
1999.7.146

48. Garden
1879–80
One of "Twenty-Six Etchings" (Second Venice Set)
Etching and drypoint
Laid paper
Watermark: RK, with possibly arms of Amsterdam
Sheet, trimmed to plate: 12 x 9 1/2 in. (305 x 241 mm)
Signed, recto, lower left in plate: artist's monogram (butterfly); in graphite, lower left on tab: artist's monogram (butterfly) and "imp."
Marks, verso, in graphite, lower left: "No 40"; "16" in a circle
Kennedy 210 viii/VIII; Mansfield 207
Provenance: Christies, New York, sale of November 5, 1991; Adolph Weil, Jr., Montgomery, Alabama
Montgomery Museum of Fine Arts, Gift of Jean K. Weil in memory of Adolph "Bucks" Weil, Jr.
1999.7.147

49. Long Venice
1879–80
One of "Twenty-Six Etchings" (Second Venice Set)
Etching and drypoint
Laid paper
Watermark: "HW Schoen" (Chicago 270)
Sheet, trimmed to plate: 5 x 12 1/4 in. (127 x 311 mm)
Signed, recto, lower left in plate: artist's monogram (butterfly); in graphite, lower left on tab,: artist's monogram (butterfly) and "imp."
Marks, verso, in graphite, lower left: "K.212 V"; lower right: "c. 6516"
Kennedy 212 v/V; Mansfield 209
Provenance: Sotheby's, New York, sale of May 15, 1986; Adolph Weil, Jr., Montgomery, Alabama
Montgomery Museum of Fine Arts, Gift of Jean K. Weil in memory of Adolph "Bucks" Weil, Jr.
1999.7.148

50. Fish-Shop, Venice
1879–80
Etching
Laid paper
Sheet: 6 3/16 x 9 3/8 in. (157 x 238 mm); image: 5 1/16 x 8 5/8 in. (129 x 219 mm)
Signed, recto, center left in plate: artist's monogram (butterfly)
Marks, verso, in graphite, lower right: "18924"; collector stamp in ink, center right: a trefoil
Kennedy 218 v/VII; Mansfield 215
Provenance: Sotheby's, New York, sale of May 15, 1986; Adolph Weil, Jr., Montgomery, Alabama
Montgomery Museum of Fine Arts, Gift of Jean K. Weil in memory of Adolph "Bucks" Weil, Jr.
1999.7.149

51. Wheelwright
1879–80
One of "Twenty-Six Etchings" (Second Venice Set)
Etching
Laid paper
Sheet, trimmed to plate: 5 1/16 x 7 in. (133 x 178 mm)
Signed, recto lower left in plate: artist's monogram (butterfly); in graphite, lower left on tab: artist's monogram (butterfly), and "imp."
Marks, verso, in graphite, lower left: "c 7597"; bottom center: illegible letters; lower right, "a. 9197; W 162; [3 illegible words, possibly "finest proof taken"] / CD"; collector stamp in ink, lower right on tab: initials "HHB" (Lugt 2936)
Kennedy 233 v/V; Mansfield 230
Provenance: Henry Harper Benedict, New York, 1919; Adolph Weil, Jr., Montgomery, Alabama
Montgomery Museum of Fine Arts, Gift of Mr. and Mrs. Adolph Weil, Jr. in memory of Mr. and Mrs. Adolph Weil, Sr.
1992.2.13

52. T. A. Nash's Fruit-Shop
ca. 1886
Etching
Japanese paper
Sheet, trimmed to plate: 6 15/16 x 4 15/16 in. (176 x 125 mm)
Signed, recto, upper right in plate: artist's monogram (butterfly); in graphite, lower left on tab: artist's monogram (butterfly) and "imp."
Marks, verso, in graphite, lower left: "a 83060"; lower right: "EVO"; upper center: "20" in a circle
Kennedy 263 iv/IV; Mansfield 260
Provenance: Frederick Keppel, New York; Kennedy Galleries, New York; Sotheby's New York, sale 5853, May 11–12, 1989, lot 301; Adolph Weil, Jr., Montgomery, Alabama
Montgomery Museum of Fine Arts, Gift of Mr. and Mrs. Adolph Weil, Jr., in memory of Mr. and Mrs. Adolph Weil, Sr.
1992.2.14

53. The Fish-Shop, Busy Chelsea

ca. 1884–86

Etching

Laid paper

Sheet, trimmed to plate: 5 1/2 x 8 9/16 in. (140 x 218 mm)

Signed, recto, upper left in plate: artist's monogram (butterfly); in graphite, lower left on tab: artist's monogram (butterfly) and "imp."

Marks, verso, in graphite, lower left: "a41835"; lower right: "Fish Shop, Busy Chelsea"

Kennedy 264 i/II; Mansfield 259

Provenance: Kennedy Galleries, New York; Adolph Weil, Jr., Montgomery, Alabama

Montgomery Museum of Fine Arts, Gift of Mr. and Mrs. Adolph Weil, Jr., in memory of Mr. and Mrs. Adolph Weil, Sr.

1992.2.15

54. Grand' Place, Brussels

1887

Etching

Laid paper

Watermark: "Pro Patria" (Chicago 331)

Sheet, trimmed to plate: 8 11/16 x 5 5/8 in. (220 x 143 mm)

Signed, recto, center right in plate: artist's monogram (butterfly); in graphite, lower left on tab: artist's monogram (butterfly) and "imp."; verso, in graphite, lower right: artist's monogram (butterfly)

Marks, verso, in graphite, lower left: "W [two illegible words] /No. 19"; bottom center: "12638" and "33641"; lower right: "1st state"

Kennedy 362 only state; Mansfield 354

Provenance: Adolph Weil, Jr., Montgomery, Alabama

Montgomery Museum of Fine Arts, Gift of Mr. and Mrs. Adolph Weil, Jr., in memory of Mr. and Mrs. Adolph Weil, Sr.

1992.2.16

55. Long House—Dyer's—Amsterdam

1889

Etching

Japanese paper

Sheet, trimmed to plate: 6 1/2 x 10 11/16 in. (165 x 271 mm)

Signed, recto, in graphite, lower right on tab: artist's monogram (butterfly) and "imp."

Marks, verso, in graphite, lower left: "NK[?] 30696"; bottom center, collector stamps in ink: "Scholle" (Lugt 2923a); a crown above "V" and "R" in an oval (Lugt 2535)

Kennedy 406 iii/III; Mansfield 408

Provenance: Bibliotheque Royale de Windsor, London; Albert W. Scholle, New York; Sotheby's, New York, sale of November 11, 1982; Adolph Weil, Jr., Montgomery, Alabama

Montgomery Museum of Fine Arts, Gift of Jean K. Weil in memory of Adolph "Bucks" Weil, Jr.

1999.7.150

56. Limehouse

1878

Lithotint

Japanese paper

Sheet: 7 5/8 x 11 1/16 in. (194 x 281 mm); image: 6 3/4 x 10 1/2 in. (171 x 268 mm)

Signed, recto, lower right in plate: artist's monogram (butterfly); in graphite, lower left: artist's monogram (butterfly)

Marks, verso, in graphite, lower left: "A20467"

Chicago 7 2/3; Way 4; Levy 8; not from published "Notes"

Provenance: Kennedy Galleries, New York, October 9, 1976; Adolph Weil, Jr., Montgomery, Alabama

Montgomery Museum of Fine Arts, Gift of Jean K. Weil in memory of Adolph "Bucks" Weil, Jr.

1999.7.151

57. Nocturne

1878

Lithotint

Wove proofing paper

Sheet: 7 5/8 x 11 in. (194 x 279 mm); image: 6 13/16 x 10 1/2 in. (173 x 267 mm)

Signed, recto, lower right in plate: artist's monogram (butterfly); in graphite, lower right: artist's monogram (butterfly)

Marks, verso, in graphite, lower left corner: "Way 5 I" and "c.17816"; lower right: "C2720." and "Museum Mt. 20 x 15 1/4"

Chicago 8 1/2; Way 5; Levy 10; proof state, not published

Provenance: Adolph Weil, Jr., Montgomery, Alabama

Montgomery Museum of Fine Arts, Gift of Jean K. Weil in memory of Adolph "Bucks" Weil, Jr.

1999.7.152

58. Old Battersea Bridge

1879

Lithograph

Laid paper

Watermark: fortune figure with Van Gelder Zonen countermark (Chicago 309)

Sheet: 11 1/8 x 17 7/8 in. (283 x 454 mm); image: 5 7/8 x 13 1/4 in. (149 x 337 mm)

Signed, recto, center left in plate: artist's monogram (butterfly); in graphite, lower left: artist's monogram (butterfly)

Marks, recto, in graphite, lower left: "W.12" bottom center: "OLD BATTERSEA BRIDGE W 12"

Marks, verso, in graphite, lower left: "Old Battersea Bridge W12"; collector stamp in ink, lower left: "BP" in a square (Lugt 406)

Chicago 18 2/2; Way 12; Levy 24

Provenance: Rosalind Birnie Philip, London; Adolph Weil, Jr., Montgomery, Alabama

Montgomery Museum of Fine Arts, Gift of Mr. and Mrs. Adolph Weil, Jr., in memory of Mr. and Mrs. Adolph Weil, Sr.

1992.2.17

59. Vitré: The Canal

1893

Lithograph

Laid paper

Watermark: "D & C Blauw" (partial) (Chicago 50, 315)

Sheet: 14 3/8 x 8 3/8 in. (365 x 213 mm); image: 9 1/4 x 6 in. (235 x 152 mm)

Signed, recto, center right in plate: artist's monogram (butterfly)

Marks, recto, in graphite, lower left: "W39"

Chicago 63 only state; Way 39; Levy 65

Provenance: Adolph Weil, Jr., Montgomery, Alabama

Montgomery Museum of Fine Arts, Gift of Mr. and Mrs. Adolph Weil, Jr., in memory of Mr. and Mrs. Adolph Weil, Sr.

1992.2.18

60. The Smith, Passage du Dragon

1894

Lithograph

Wove paper

Sheet: 11 3/8 x 8 7/8 in. (289 x 225 mm); image: 10 7/8 x 7 in. (276 x 178 mm)

Signed, recto, center left in plate: artist's monogram (butterfly); in graphite, lower right: artist's monogram (butterfly)

Marks, verso, in graphite, lower left: "a 38399" and "a 9364"; collector stamp in ink, lower left: "HHB" (Lugt 1298)

Chicago 103 ii/III; Way 73; Levy 109

Provenance: H.H. Benedict, New York; Kennedy Galleries, New York; Adolph Weil Jr., Montgomery, Alabama

Montgomery Museum of Fine Arts, Gift of Mr. and Mrs. Adolph Weil, Jr., in memory of Mr. and Mrs. Adolph Weil, Sr.

1992.2.19

61. Evening, Little Waterloo Bridge

1896

Lithograph

Japanese paper

Sheet: 7 3/4 x 10 5/8 in. (197 x 270 mm); image: 3 1/2 x 7 1/2 in. (89 x 191 mm)

Signed, recto, lower right in plate: artist's monogram (butterfly)

Marks, recto, in graphite, lower left: "W.165"; verso, in graphite, lower right: "W119"; collector stamp in ink, lower left: "BP" in a square (Lugt 406)

Chicago 155 ii/II; Way 119; Levy 165

Provenance: Rosalind Birnie Philip, London; Adolph Weil, Jr., Montgomery, Alabama.

Montgomery Museum of Fine Arts, Gift of Mr. and Mrs. Adolph Weil, Jr., in memory of Mr. and Mrs. Adolph Weil, Sr.

1992.2.20

62. Waterloo Bridge

1896

Lithograph

Laid paper

Watermark: fortune figure with Van Gelder Zonen countermark (Chicago 309)

Sheet: 11 3/16 x 9 in. (284 x 229 mm); image: 7 x 5 in. (178 x 127 mm)

Signed, recto, lower right in plate: artist's monogram (butterfly)

Marks, recto, in graphite, lower left: "Waterloo Bridge W 123"; lower left: "W123/ c5571"

Marks, verso, in graphite, lower left: "c 7466"; bottom center: "way 123"; lower right: "B.1241" and "~~B.279~~"; collector stamp in ink, lower right: "T.R.W." in a rectangle (Lugt 2456)

Chicago 156 only state; Way 123; Levy 177

Provenance: Thomas Robert Way, London; Adolph Weil, Jr., Montgomery, Alabama

Montgomery Museum of Fine Arts, Gift of Mr. and Mrs. Adolph Weil, Jr., in memory of Mr. and Mrs. Adolph Weil, Sr.

1992.2.21

63. The Thames

1896

Lithotint

Wove proofing paper

Sheet: 12 x 9 1/4 in. (305 x 235 mm); image: 10 1/2 x 7 3/4 in. (267 x 197 mm)

Signed, recto, lower right in plate: artist's monogram (butterfly); verso, in graphite, lower right: artist's monogram (butterfly)

Marks, verso, lower left: "122014.1 OUXX / ~~a37129~~; "W125II/III The Thames"

Chicago 161 2/3; Way 125; Levy 179

Provenance: Kennedy Galleries, New York, 1980; Adolph Weil, Jr., Montgomery, Alabama

Montgomery Museum of Fine Arts, Gift of Jean K. Weil in memory of Adolph "Bucks" Weil, Jr.

1999.7.153

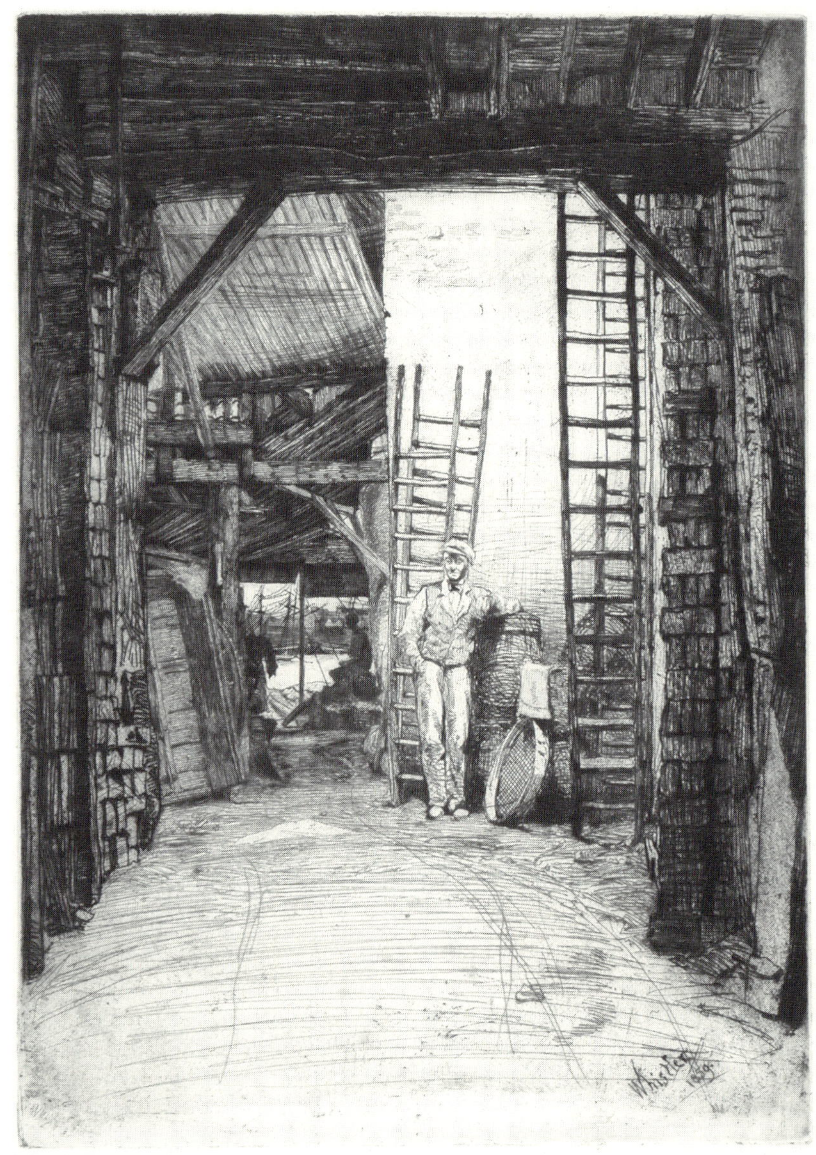

The Lime-Burner, 1859
Etching on laid paper
14 1/2 x 9 3/16 in.
Gift of Mr. and Mrs. Adolph Weil, Jr., in memory of Mr. and Mrs. Adolph Weil, Sr.
1984.17.8

Selected Bibliography

Andrew, William W. *Otto H. Bacher.* 1935. Reprint. Madison, Wisconsin: Education Industries, 1973.

Bacher, Otto H. *With Whistler in Venice.* New York: Century Company, 1908.

Black, Peter. *Copper into Gold: Whistler and Nineteenth-Century Printmaking.* Exhibition catalogue. Glasgow: Hunterian Art Gallery, University of Glasgow, 2003.

[Chicago.]
Harriet Stratis and Martha Tedeschi, gen. eds. *The Lithographs of James McNeill Whistler.* Volume 1: *A Catalogue Raisonné* by Martha Tedeschi, Nesta Spink, Harriet Stratis, with Britt Salvesen and Katherine Lochnan. Volume 2: *Correspondence and Technical Studies* (including Watermarks) edited by Nicolas Smale. Chicago: Art Institute of Chicago/Arie and Ida Crown Memorial, 1998.

Curry, David Park. *James McNeill Whistler at the Freer Gallery of Art.* Exhibition catalogue. Washington, D.C.: Freer Gallery of Art, Smithsonian Institution; New York: W. W. Norton, 1984.

——. *James McNeill Whistler: Uneasy Pieces.* Exhibition catalogue. Richmond: Virginia Museum of Fine Arts/Quantuck Lane Press; New York: W.W. Norton, 2004.

Denker, Eric. *In Pursuit of the Butterfly: Portraits of James McNeill Whistler.* Exhibition catalogue. Washington, D.C.: National Portrait Gallery/University of Washington Press, 1995.

———. *Whistler and His Circle in Venice.* Exhibition catalogue. London: Merrell; Washington, D.C.: Corcoran Gallery of Art, 2003.

Dorment, Richard, and Margaret F. MacDonald with Nicolai Cikovsky, Jr., Ruth Fine, and Geneviève Lacambre. *James McNeill Whistler.* Exhibition catalogue. London: Tate Gallery; New York: Harry N. Abrams, 1994.

Getscher, Robert H. "Whistler and Venice." Ph.D. dissertation, Case Western Reserve University, 1970.

———. *The Stamp of Whistler.* Exhibition catalogue. Oberlin, Ohio: Allan Memorial Art Museum, 1977.

Grieve, Alastair. *Whistler's Venice.* New Haven: Yale University Press/Paul Mellon Centre for Studies in British Art, 2000.

Honour, Hugh, and John Fleming. *The Venetian Hours of Henry James, Whistler, and Sargent.* London: Walker Books; Boston: Little, Brown/Bulfinch Press, 1991.

House, John, Petra Ten-Doesschate Chu, Jennifer Hardin. *Monet's London: Artists' Reflections on the Thames, 1859–1914.* Exhibition catalogue. Ghent, Belgium: Distributed Art Publications, 2005.

Kennedy, Edward G. *The Etched Work of Whistler: Illustrated by Reproduction in Collotype of the Different States of the Plates.* Five volumes. New York: Grolier Club/DeVinne Press, 1910.

Levy, Mervyn. *Whistler Lithographs: A Catalogue Raisonné.* London: Jupiter Books, 1975.

Lochnan, Katharine A. *The Etchings of James McNeill Whistler.* New Haven and London: Yale University Press, 1984.

———. *Turner, Whistler, Monet.* Exhibition catalogue. Toronto: Art Gallery of Ontario/Tate Publishing: New York: Harry N. Abrams, 2004.

———. "Whistler's Etchings and the Sources of His Etching Style, 1855–1880." PhD diss., Courtauld Institute, 1982.

Lovell, Margaretta M. *Venice: The American View, 1860–1920.* Exhibition catalogue. San Francisco: Fine Arts Museums of San Francisco, 1984.

Lugt, Fritz. *Les Marques de collections de dessins et d'estampes.* Amsterdam: Vereenigde Drukkerijen, 1921.

MacDonald, Margaret F. *James McNeill Whistler: Drawings, Pastels, and Watercolours; A Catalogue Raisonné.* New Haven and London: Yale University Press/Paul Mellon Centre for Studies in British Art, 1995.

———. *Palaces in the Night: Whistler in Venice.* Aldershot, Hampshire: Lund Humphries; Berkeley: University of California Press, 2001.

———. *James McNeill Whistler: The Venetian Etchings.* Exhibition catalogue. London: Art Partnerships International, 2001.

MacNamara, Carole, and John Siewert. *Whistler: Prosaic Views, Poetic Vision; Works on Paper from the University of Michigan Museum of Art.* Exhibition catalogue. Ann Arbor: University of Michigan Museum of Art; New York: Thames and Hudson, 1994.

Mansfield, Howard. *A Descriptive Catalogue of the Etchings and Dry-points of James Abbott McNeill Whistler.* Chicago: Caxton Club, 1909.

Menpes, Dorothy, and Mortimer Menpes. *Venice.* London: A & C Black, 1904.

Menpes, Mortimer. *Whistler as I Knew Him.* London: A.C. Black, 1904.

Merrill, Linda. *A Pot of Paint: Aesthetics on Trial in* Whistler v Ruskin. Washington, D. C. & London: Smithsonian Institution Press/Freer Gallery of Art, 1992.

Merrill, Linda, with Robyn Asleson, Lee Glazer, Lacey Taylor Jordan, John Siewert, Marc Simpson, and Sylvia Yount. *After Whistler: The Artist and His Influence on American Painting.* Exhibition catalogue. New Haven: Yale University Press; Atlanta: High Museum of Art, 2003.

Pennell, Elizabeth Robins. *Nights: Rome, Venice in the Aesthetic Eighties; London, Paris in the Fighting Nineties.* London: J. B. Lippincott Company, 1916.

Pennell, Elizabeth Robins, and Joseph Pennell. *The Life of James McNeill Whistler.* Two volumes. London: William Heinemann; Philadelphia: J. B. Lippincott Company, 1908.

———. *The Life of James McNeill Whistler.* New & revised 5th edition. London: William Heinemann; Philadelphia: J. B. Lippincott Company, 1911.

———. *The Whistler Journal.* Philadelphia: J. B. Lippincott Company, 1921.

Robins, Anna Gruetzner, ed. *Walter Sickert: The Complete Writings on Art.* Oxford and New York: Oxford University Press, 2000.

Spencer, Robin, ed. *Whistler: A Retrospective.* New York: Hugh Lauter Levin Associates, 1989.

Stratis, Harriet, & Martha Tedeschi. See Chicago, or see, Tedeschi, Martha et al.

Tedeschi, Martha, Nesta Spink, Harriet Stratis, with Britt Salvesen and Katherine Lochnan. *A Catalogue Raisonné.* Volume 1 of *The Lithographs of James McNeill Whistler,* Harriet Stratis and Martha Tedeschi, gen. eds. Chicago: Art Institute of Chicago/Arie and Ida Crown Memorial, 1998.

Thorp, Nigel, ed. *Whistler on Art: Selected Letters and Writings, 1849–1903, of James McNeill Whistler.* Glasgow: Centre for Whistler Studies, University of Glasgow; Washington, D.C.: Smithsonian Institution Press, 1994.

Way, Thomas Robert. *Memories of J. M. Whistler the Artist.* London: John Lane; New York: John Lane Company, 1912.

Way, Thomas Robert, and G. R. Dennis. *The Art of James McNeill Whistler: An Appreciation.* London: G. Bell, 1903.

Whistler, James McNeill. *The Gentle Art of Making Enemies.* London: William Heinemann, 1890.

Young, Andrew McLaren, Margaret F. MacDonald, and Robin Spencer, with Hamish Miles. *The Paintings of James McNeill Whistler.* Two volumes. New Haven and London: Yale University Press/Paul Mellon Centre for Studies in British Art, 1980.